# WORKING SMARTER, NOT JUST HARDER

# WORKING SMARTER, NOT JUST HARDER

THREE SENSIBLE STRATEGIES FOR SUCCEEDING IN COLLEGE...AND LIFE

Karl W. Reid, Ed.D.

ISBN: 0692834907
ISBN 13: 9780692834909
Library of Congress Control Number: 2017900694
Karl W. Reid,Silver Spring,MARYLAND

# DEDICATION

*To my father who taught me how to dream, and my sister who showed me what dreams can achieve.*

*Kenneth W. Reid*
*1927-1994*


*Monique Reid Berryhill*
*1956-2005*

# ACKNOWLEDGEMENTS

THE BIBLICAL WRITER to the Hebrews wrote, "Therefore, since we are surrounded by such a great cloud of witnesses...let us run with perseverance the race marked out for us" (Hebrews 12:1).

I'm so grateful for my "cloud of witnesses" who've supported and inspired me throughout this journey. My wife, Andrea, is an endless source of inspiration especially over the past five years while I was writing and rewriting this book. Our children, Jasmine, Drew, and Miles, have exemplified unconditional love despite my frequent physical and emotional absences during this period. My parents, Joyce and the late Kenneth Reid, instilled in me big dreams and the zeal to share the benefits of high-quality education with the most marginalized among us. My siblings, Keith, Kendrick, and my late sister Monique, have always been models of excellence who've cheered me on from afar. I am also grateful for my "mother-in-love", Gloria Robinson, who ignited my passion to pursue education advocacy when she prophetically sent me Jonathan Kozol's "Savage Inequalities" back in 1991. My dear pastors, Gideon Thompson, Ray Hammond, and Matthew Watley, provided inspired spiritual care while showing me "The Way" to discover and pursue my purpose. Thanks to Rick Horowitz of Prime Prose, LLC and Eric Addison of Addison Editorial Services, LLC, for their expertise in helping to bring this manuscript to life and make it more accessible to its intended audiences. I'm very grateful to my NSBE family, which has given me a platform to express my true calling. And most importantly, I thank God in whom I live, and move, and have my being (Acts 17:28).

# TABLE OF CONTENTS

# INTRODUCTION

I FELT DUMB. So will you.

I conquered that feeling. So can you.

Before I went to college, I was a great student. My parents and siblings marveled at how easily academic success came to me. My teachers and my parents lathered me with praise, telling me I was a smart kid. And I believed it. When I graduated from a highly ranked high school in the top 10 percent of my class, I felt I was on a glide path to success, destined to meet the high expectations that had been set for me and reap the rewards that came with it.

That is, of course, until I arrived at college.

In my first few classes there, I was confronted with the reality that I didn't understand anything going on in lecture. I was confused even when it came to subjects I had taken in high school. My first exam grade was abysmal, and it was a class in my major!

It was the first time I'd ever felt so disoriented. I marveled at how so many of my classmates could have a dialogue with the professor when I could barely formulate a basic question.

Successful in high school, then struggling in college: I was hardly the only student facing this predicament. And what was true then is just as true now — successful high-school grads can still "hit the wall" when they move to the next level.

As with every student, my background wasn't particularly unique: I grew up middle class, the third child in a mostly working-class community in Long Island, N.Y. Neither of my parents earned college degrees; my mother went right to work after high school. I idolized my older brother, who graduated from MIT as a chemical engineer. I am African American. Throughout my education, I'd seen many of my classmates underperform academically after showing great talent in their early years, and I'd often wondered why.

But almost everyone struggles in college. If you're like most students, you'll have your first "academic wake-up call" in the fall semester of your freshman year. Some of you who had stronger preparation in high school may skate through that first semester, but you'll hit that wall when you're introduced to new material in the spring. Regardless of when it happens, you will be challenged. If struggle hasn't come your way yet, you're either in a school or major that's not challenging you enough (and you should consider transferring), or you should get ready, because it's about to happen.

Your college entrance scores are a poor predictor of whether you'll earn your degree. Barely more than half of all college students earn a four-year degree within six years of entering as freshmen, and 28 percent don't return after their first year! If you're a male or a person of color — African American, Native American or Latino — your odds of obtaining a bachelor's degree in six years are even worse.

And success is not only about how hard you study, either. Your parents and teachers have probably told you repeatedly to "Study harder!" Even in college, when you get a poor grade or fail to grasp the work, a professor or teaching assistant will offer that sage advice: "Study harder!" It's true: Students need to work harder by putting in more hours to prepare for class. According to one recent study, the average number of hours college students spend doing schoolwork outside of the classroom has dwindled over the past 50 years, from 24 hours per week to only 15.

But putting in more time doesn't always translate into better grades or deeper learning. (You may have already realized this.)

If I asked you, "What does 'Study harder' look like?" you probably would conjure images of students working diligently in their dorm room — say, burning the midnight oil to finish a paper. Others of you might envision all-night cramming sessions with your friends.

Unfortunately, these industrious images aren't always put into practice. But even when they are, many students discover that their efforts are insufficient. They're simply not effective.

"Effective" is the operative word here. Only about half of all college students recently polled said they had developed *effective* study habits in college. The issue, I've come to understand, is not only about working longer or harder: It's about learning how to *work smarter*.

Vince Lombardi, the late Hall of Fame coach of the Green Bay Packers, famously said, "The only place that success comes before work is in the dictionary." Unless you're attending a college where you're not being challenged, I know you're working hard, or at least you believe you are. However, if you're like I was, your hard work is not getting the results you expect. It's not as effective as you want it to be — or as you need it to be.

It took me a while to learn the steps that helped me to be successful. Like water finding its own level, I had to discover an approach to learning that worked for me. Fortunately, during my first semester in college, I discovered that new approach. I had to. Had I not learned *how to learn*, I don't know where I'd be today, and I certainly wouldn't have been able to write this book to help you.

Ultimately, I've had great success: two degrees in engineering from MIT, a doctorate in education and a fruitful career — first in the software industry, then in higher education, and now as executive director of a professional society for engineers. But it didn't come easily. You may find yourself facing some of the very same hurdles I faced. You don't have to face them alone.

This book guides you through the learning approach that helped turn things around for me as an undergraduate, an approach that I refined as a doctoral student, a freshman advisor and a college dean. It will help you get smarter. Not only smarter in knowing the material but smarter in the way you approach your work.

This book provides a model, one that you'll adapt to your own style and your own situation. And it offers a mindset — a way of thinking — that will underpin those strategies as you adapt them to meet your particular needs.

Here's my central point: It's time to change how you think about your academic abilities and work, the relationships you build to help you approach that work, and the steps you take to help you master that work. Those changes, I've discovered, make all the difference between successful and unsuccessful students. I call these changes *"shifts,"* because most students have to dramatically *shift* their thinking and their actions in college to succeed.

You may have noticed this already, and if you haven't, you almost certainly will: The learning strategies that used to work in high school no longer work in college. Like driving in the wrong gear on the highway, doing the same thing harder and for longer periods of time won't necessarily get the job done. Your intellectual engine is revving at high RPMs, but you're still not moving fast enough on the college superhighway. Other students are whizzing by you. You need to shift gears.

This book is all about how to shift gears. In the next few chapters, I'll show you how making three specific "shifts" will help you succeed in college:

The first one, *The Attitude Shift*, focuses on developing that new mindset about your intellectual ability, and on the importance of confidence and how to rebuild it, especially after you suffer setbacks. That's Chapter II.

*The Connections Shift* (Chapter III) shows how important it is to engage your faculty members and peers on campus, and how to do it. This chapter teaches you how to approach teachers, even if you're shy, and how to utilize study groups of fellow students to maximize your learning.

And finally, *The Behavior Shift* (Chapter IV) offers practical steps for improving your grades and deepening your learning. This chapter provides both the rationale behind, and the steps toward, developing the kind of comprehensive approach that has helped countless students succeed.

By applying these "shifts," you'll learn how to work smarter, and you'll see your grades and overall satisfaction with your performance dramatically improve.

In each of these three chapters, I also list some "Smart Shift Takeaways," designed as "ticklers," or reminders. When baseball players go through hitting slumps, they watch video of themselves during a hot streak. Similarly, these takeaways are designed to remind you about your successful steps until you can build up your "muscle memory" and make them consistently your own.

A word of caution: Don't approach this book like you're reading the "CliffsNotes" of a work of literature. You know what I mean. When I was in school, I had friends who avoided reading the assigned literature and instead bought and read the summaries. These summaries are even easier to find today, on the internet, and they're a tempting shortcut to doing the real work. Bad move. You can't short-circuit learning.

To get everything out of a novel — the tone, the nuance of the dialogue and the underlying back-stories — you have to read the whole book. Similarly, to fully learn how to achieve success in college, you have to start at the beginning.

"Just tell me what I need to *do!*" you may be thinking. But for *The Behavior Shift* to stick, you'll first have to understand and apply *The Attitude Shift* and *The Connections Shift*. When you're building a structure to sustain you throughout your academic life, and even beyond, it's essential to lay a strong foundation.

For those of you interested in examining the research behind these strategies, peruse the article I've included in the appendix.

Are you up to the challenge? I hope you are, because the benefits of meeting the challenge of all three shifts are great, not only in college but throughout your life. In fact, the principles embedded in the three shifts — internalizing empowering attitudes, making strategic connections, and learning how to learn effectively — are applicable whether you're in high school, college, or the workplace.

Before I turn in more detail to the three shifts, I'll share a bit of my own story: how I struggled as a first-year college student and how I responded to the challenge. That struggle, and my response, became the kernel for this book: a process I've dubbed *The Deep Dive Learning Approach*. In the course of writing the book, I've shared the information in this next chapter with hundreds of high school and college students and faculty members around the country. The feedback has been universally positive. One freshman enthusiastically wrote to tell me that he could relate to my story and asked whether he might share it with his classmates. A math professor asked to share it with freshman counselors at his college. If you find the strategies helpful, please share this book with others. Better yet, tell them to buy a copy of their own!

Two final notes: This book is designed to help all students, but certain groups will find the approach and stories most relevant. Although all high-school and college students, as well as early- career professionals, will gain considerable insight from the approach I'll introduce, it may be especially useful for those who are taking quantitative courses such as mathematics, physics, chemistry, engineering, economics and finance. Even so, the chapters on *The Attitude Shift* and *The Connections Shift* will appeal to all students, regardless of their courses or major.

Similarly, because I am an African American who attended a predominantly white university, and because my research has focused on the successful experiences of minority students, I write from the perspective of a person of color. But again, although this book will be particularly instructive to those who belong to racial or ethnic minorities, the lessons learned can be applied to all students, regardless of their race or ethnicity.

I mentioned in my very first lines that every student struggles at some point in college. This book is designed to help every student face down that challenge, overcome that struggle and learn to work smarter.

I did it, and you can do it, too.

Let's get started.

# CHAPTER 1

## OVERCOMING STRUGGLES

### MY EARLY YEARS

I WAS ALWAYS a good student in elementary and high school. Diligent and focused, I took my schooling seriously. After all, I was in a family that held a high bar for us all. My sister, Monique, the oldest of my siblings, became the valedictorian of her high school and went on to Oberlin College and then to a successful career practicing corporate law. My brother Keith, five years my elder, went to MIT after a stellar high school career, at the same high school I would eventually attend. Keith became an engineer, and then went into fulltime ministry, rising to senior administrative ranks in his church denomination. And my younger brother, Kendrick, would follow me to that same high school two years later, and then would attend Boston University and eventually become a successful executive in the cable-television industry. And I'm an executive director of a global association that promotes education, diversity and inclusion in the engineering sector.

My parents communicated high expectations for schoolwork with a delicate balance of support and correction. Unlike the recent accounts of "Tiger Moms" who punish their children when they come home with a bad grade, my parents were much more loving and supportive, but they balanced that love and support with tough standards. I recall once in third grade coming home with a 99 on an English test. (I had forgotten a comma on the punctuation section of the exam.) Although my parents were happy that I did so well, they still reminded me of their expectations. "Nice job", I remember them lovingly saying, "but what happened?"

The four of us — my sister and two brothers and me — followed career paths that my Dad cast by the sheer strength of his personality and passion. Born in New York, and raised in Jamaica, West Indies, and the Bronx, my Dad never finished college. However, like many children of immigrants, he believed deeply in the promise of education. From the many mini-lectures we received, we internalized his passion for technology, law, film and photography. When I was three years old, he taught me to say "Massachusetts Institute of Technology". I had trouble saying Massachusetts (never mind "Institute" and "Technology"), so when he'd ask what "MIT stood for", I used to simply say "mit". For my Dad, MIT was the paragon of technology and innovation, known for its rigorous curriculum, and he wanted no less for his technologically inquisitive son. (I remember sticking a stapler in an outlet to see what would happen. Thank God, my curiosity didn't kill me, but I did learn what a circuit breaker was.)

Though he was the visionary for us, his work as a police officer and later as an entrepreneur meant that he wasn't home much to monitor our schoolwork. That job went to my Mom.

My mother was born in Canada to a Barbadian family that had migrated north to work the coal mines in Nova Scotia. Though her formal education ended with a high school diploma, my Mom was the educational supervisor in our household. She scrutinized our grades, made sure we weren't watching too much television and that we were regularly practicing our musical instruments. When we were young, she used to read to us day and night. Dad, who was always on the "bleeding edge" of new technologies, recorded some of these reading sessions on his reel-to-reel recorder for posterity (or as long as those tapes held up — which wasn't very long, it turned out).

Though they were all very accomplished, my siblings thought schoolwork came more easily for me than for them. I'd work hard, but school learning was very intuitive for me, so understanding came more quickly, and without much struggle. This came back to bite me when I made it to college and the work became harder.

And it's the reason I've written this book.

## "WHITE BOY"

As a young African American boy in school and in my neighborhood, I struggled to avoid the backhanded insults that were lobbed at me from my so-called friends. They used to call me "White Boy" and "Goody" with friendly banter, this even from some of my closest friends. These words hurt, so I would do my best to deflect discussions about school when I was with my friends. We talked about and played basketball and touch football, and built and rode bicycles and mini-bikes when we got a little older, but I made sure never to bring up the subject of school. School wasn't cool.

In high school, I would threaten to dumb down my effort just to fit in, but my parents weren't having it. Here's where my Dad would help shape my aspirations. Dad would remind me that I would be going to "MIT" one day, live on Nob Hill (an exclusive neighborhood on Long Island), and be able to walk into a car dealer and purchase a car with cash.

"Your friends," he'd say, "will still be home living with their parents." See, as a New York City police officer and narcotics detective at the time, he saw daily the outcome of my friends' adult-life trajectories, which weren't as aspirational; those friends didn't aim as high. And so he often reminded us about the divergent paths that awaited us. Those mini-lectures were a constant refrain in my head when I encountered the teasing. And what's more, I had the examples of my sister Monique and my brother Keith to follow. I had no option but to resist my friends' insults and push through it. I developed my own internal dialogue about what I would become — and education was the path to get me there.

By junior year in high school, I was attending a magnet school among other kids from my low-to middle-income town. The "White Boy" label seemed to have vanished, as I was going to school with other black students who had similar high expectations and whose parents pushed them equally hard. I was coming into my own: I was heading to a competitive college, leading the "Afro-American Culture Club" in my predominantly white high school, and joining a New York City leadership development group; the Bishop's Leadership Project raised my aspirations even further while exposing me to phenomenal older men of color who attended the likes of Brown, Wesleyan, Harvard, and MIT.

## CHOOSING A COLLEGE

By senior year, I was ranked in the top 10 percent of my high school, taking two AP courses, and selected to be drum major of the marching band. I was admitted to all the colleges to which I had applied — including MIT. I was well on my way to being successful in life. Or so I thought.

I chose to attend MIT, probably because it was most familiar to me and most aligned with my engineering interests. My brother had just graduated from "the Institute", and, as I mentioned, my Dad had been grooming me to attend MIT since I was three. (I have to give it to my parents, though: They put no pressure on me when it came time for me to make the decision. My Dad and my Mom allowed me to make the decision I thought was best for me.)

While my high school had a lot going for it, because of a quirk in the curriculum, I had graduated without taking chemistry or biology; my science requirements had been satisfied with electronics and computer-science courses. This gap in my education, as I'll explain later, would prove to be a blessing — and a curse.

Still, bolstered by the great momentum from high school and the love and support of family and mentors, I walked into college with all of the confidence in the world. A confidence that was soon shattered.

## THE TRANSITION TO COLLEGE

Unbeknownst to me, the MIT admissions officers must have thought that the science deficits in my high school record were a cause for concern, and for early assistance. They invited me to participate in a "bridge" program. Project Interphase was a seven-week summer academic program for admitted freshmen of color (and later for other similarly underprepared students), to help ease their transition to college. We took freshman-level calculus, physics, chemistry, writing, and computer science. The classes, which were designed to mimic and prepare us for the first year of college, were taught both by MIT professors and graduate students. The program quickly exposed the gaps in my preparation; the pace of the classes was way beyond my ability to comprehend. I remember sitting in one of the first physics classes that summer and feeling overwhelmed. I realized I was out of my league when I couldn't even answer the professor's question when the question was, "Do you have a question?"

What made matters worse was the feeling of inadequacy when others *could* answer the questions. In fact, they would answer questions...with questions, demonstrating a command of the material I severely lacked. I barely understood the terminology being bandied between professor and student.

The only class in which I felt somewhat competent was calculus, largely because it was closest in content to what I had learned in high school. Even the writing course was foreign to me. Despite my AP English class my senior year, I never had to read, analyze, and write as much as I was being required to do in this short, seven-week program.

My first physics "problem set" — the homework assignment for this course — was a disaster. That was true for chemistry as well. Each problem set was merely five or six problems long, but it took days to finish. Except for the help of a group of fellow students, I probably wouldn't have turned anything in, and certainly nothing complete. Instead, with their help, I did turn in my first problem sets, though I didn't fully understand what I was doing. The same for my second problem set. In fact, I didn't understand a thing. And it showed on my first few exams. I never saw marks as low as I was getting. Suddenly, this smart kid was looking and feeling very dumb.

## AN IDENTITY CRISIS

I had always thought I was smart because I got good grades and work came relatively easily to me. The two were inextricably linked. Smart = good grades. Good grades = smart. But if that were true, then how could I explain my suddenly poor grades? What did my struggles to learn and understand in college mean for my identity as a successful student? If smart = good grades, then what do bad grades equal? I didn't want to explicitly answer the question, but my performance was drawing me down a vortex of self-defeatism.

Somehow I recovered just enough to pass the courses that summer. I relied heavily on study groups and relentless tutoring from the upperclassmen who served as dorm tutors. I attended every exam review, took extensive notes, and studied those notes, though not actively as I'll explain later. Unlike in high school, where it seemed I had to put in less effort than my siblings and my peers, the opposite was true in college. It seemed I had to put in much more work than everyone else. And I wondered: If I had to put this much work and rely on so many others to be average or just to get by, could I ever be successful in college?

## STUMBLING UPON A MAJOR

Despite my steep learning curve, I began to enjoy my chemistry course during the Interphase summer program. The topics resonated with my practical sensibilities. As one who used to build rockets and go-carts in the basement, and who tinkered with bicycles and mini-bike engines in the garage, I was fascinated by mechanical things. I appreciated how physical chemistry explained so much of the day-to-day phenomena I encountered: why certain materials behaved differently under a variety of conditions such as temperature, light or pressure. Chemistry (solid-state chemistry in particular) seemed to answer some of those lingering questions.

I spoke with one of my tutors — a materials science and engineering major — about my growing fascination with chemistry, and she suggested I consider her field. I hadn't heard of it before. I called my older brother Keith, who had graduated from MIT a year earlier with a degree in chemical engineering, and told him of my newfound love for chemistry, and about the conversation I had just had. If he had a chance to restart his MIT education, he replied, he would have majored in materials science and engineering, too, instead of chemical engineering. Materials science was a good balance, he said, of mechanical engineering and chemistry. His endorsement sold me: Materials science and engineering would be my major.

## THE DIFFERENCE BETWEEN *THE WHAT* AND *THE WHY*

Making that decision was one thing, but becoming proficient in the subject matter remained elusive. There is a difference between memorizing a series of steps and truly understanding how each step contributes to solving a problem. I still approached my learning by studying *The What*, but I wasn't grasping *The Why*.

At MIT and many institutions like it, it's *The Why*, not merely *The What*, that leads to innovation and understanding. I had never been taught that way. We were taught how to do something — solve a problem, analyze a passage, build a circuit — but lacked an appreciation of why we were doing it. However, any professor worth his or her weight will test students on their knowledge of *The Why*. They'll introduce a problem on the exam that is unrecognizable in order to assess your understanding of the underlying concepts. Until I grasped this reality and mastered the concepts that underlay *The What*, I always felt I was behind the eight ball.

## FRESHMAN YEAR: ANOTHER WAKEUP CALL

But having survived the summer, I went into my first semester as a freshman a little too cocky. After all, I did *reasonably well* during Project Interphase on topics that I was told would be covered again during this semester. At least I had passed, albeit with a lot of help

During the first few weeks of the fall semester, I seemed to understand what was going on in lecture, and problem sets were much simpler now that I had already covered the material during the summer.

My first exam was in physical chemistry, in my intended major, materials science and engineering. The night before the exam, the Office of Minority Education held a study break in the Tutorial Services room. They were serving ice cream, and arranged to have upperclassmen available to answer questions the freshmen had about what they'd be facing the next morning. My friends and I went for the ice cream, not the tutoring. After all, I'd just had seven summer weeks of physical chemistry, the same subject and ostensibly the same topics that I'd already learned. This was my sweet spot! I had this!

I returned to my room about 9 p.m. and opened my textbook, and my notebook. I gave the material a cursory glance. I don't recall working any problems. I browsed my graded problem sets as well, noting what I did wrong, but *precisely because my marks were less than stellar,* I didn't go through the homework assignments with a critical eye, because it would have reminded me how dumb I was. The grades on those problem sets were warning signs, but unfortunately, I missed the signs. I went to bed after no more than an hour or two of studying.

## SELF-DOUBT CREEPS IN AGAIN

The test was about as hard as they were that summer. No big deal. I had passed chemistry in Project Interphase, and I was sure I passed this exam as well. I was flummoxed when I got my grade back: a 38! It felt like I was hit by a truck. What just happened? After all, I had sat through the start of the fall semester listening to topics that were being re-taught. While some of my friends did as poorly as I did, others did better, in the 50s. More startling was the realization that many more in the class scored in the 80s and 90s.

Suddenly, I was awash in self-doubt again, just as I was at the beginning of the summer. Maybe MIT was not for me. I mean, how could I have scored a 38 while others earned 80s and 90s? The tables had been turned from my high school days; I was no longer on top. Worse, I didn't know why I did so poorly, except for the lingering thought that I wasn't as smart as everyone had made me believe.

When the exams were returned, the teaching assistant informed us that the class average was 55, and the standard deviation was 19. This meant that two-thirds of the class scored between 36 and 74 — that is, from 19 points below to 19 points above the class average. At the time, particularly for the freshman courses, if you scored within and above the standard deviation, you passed. (Many colleges including mine have abandoned this practice of "grading on a curve.") In other words, my 38, which was two points within the range, was a passing score! I was elated. I had passed my first freshman exam…with a 38! Mediocrity never felt so good.

As you can see, my early MIT career was an emotional rollercoaster. That 38 in physical chemistry was a sharp drop, but finding out that I had passed was an emotional uplift.

It turned out to be only a temporary one.

## A THREAT: MY CATALYST FOR WORKING SMARTER

A short time later, by chance (though I don't believe in chance) I bumped into my physical chemistry professor, August Witt. He was an Austrian with a pronounced German accent that was very intimidating. Professor Witt asked me how I did on his first exam. I got a 38, I told him, and with a smile on my face fresh off the recent revelation, I declared, "But I passed!"

He did not share my enthusiasm. He moved in close, typical of Europeans with their different sense of personal space — a proximity that is typically uncomfortable for us Americans, and extremely uncomfortable for an 18-year-old kid. Nearly nose to nose, he looked me in the eyes and threatened me with words that changed my MIT trajectory.

"Young man," he said with a stern voice, "if you don't start to work harder in this class, you will fail." Down went the emotional coaster again. I was devastated and embarrassed. His words felt like a punch in the gut, more poignant and painful than getting the 38 in the first place. And I felt the impact even more because I was not doing especially well in physics either. (I was doing OK in calculus, but I wasn't knocking it out of the park.)

Years later, when I had maturity behind me, I reflected on Professor Witt's threat. He forcefully and compellingly sent two messages. Here was one of the most feared and renowned professors conveying to me, a middle class Black kid from Roosevelt, Long Island, in blunt terms that he expected better of me. That was the first message. He also gave me a roadmap to success: Work harder. I needed to get out of the morass of mediocrity, and Professor Witt laid down the gauntlet, but also provided a way out.

I didn't process the full meaning of his message at the time. I do remember that the dominant emotion, at that seminal moment in the hallway of Building 13, was fear of failure. That threat was a catalyst for me. I made a commitment to myself that I would do better. I had to. My high school approach wasn't working for me in college, and if I was going to survive, I had to approach my work differently. I had to make a shift. I was stuck in second gear.

## TOUCHED BY AN ANGEL

Professor Witt wasn't the only adult at MIT who helped me overcome my early stumbles. I thank God, too, for my freshman advisor, Dr. Clarence Williams. Dr. Williams had been at MIT for more than a decade when I entered my freshman year, serving as special assistant to the president and an ombudsperson. He had known my older brother who also attended MIT so he knew I came from good stock. Dr. Williams had high expectations for me, and never failed to communicate them. During this period, though he didn't offer specific advice, he reminded me that

MIT *was* the place for me, and that I would be successful, but I had to find my way. Probably without him even knowing it, he filled me with a sense of "belongingness" which is so essential to success in college. He saw my potential as a student and as a student leader.

Though in subsequent years he was no longer my official advisor, he continued to counsel me through my MIT career, and well afterward... for 25 years, even after he retired. When my travels bring me to his region of the country, I check in on "Clarence," particularly when I need to be reminded of who I am and what I can become.

There's an important lesson in that experience: Find adults in college who can speak into your life, who know your capabilities and, more importantly, who can see your potential. Throughout my time at MIT and in later life, I met other "Clarences" who also played crucial roles in my development.

Your path forward will be much smoother with valuable guides like these to help encourage you along the way.

## I BEGAN BY CHANGING MY SURROUNDINGS

My first task was to translate those words of encouragement and high expectations from people I respected into concrete action. I started close to home — literally.

I lived in an all-male section of the MIT dorm called Chocolate City, or "CC." CC was founded by a group of African American upperclassmen when the dormitory opened in 1975. The name would be based on the title song of a Parliament/Funkadelic album; Chocolate City was the nickname for Washington, DC, because of its majority-black population. The goal of the "CC" dorm was to establish a culturally safe place for the 28 young black men who lived there.

CC had a regional reputation for its parties and the beautiful young college women who frequented the place, some of whom stayed for days at a time as "guests." Though we had the off-campus attraction of being MIT students with promising futures, on campus we were not known for our academic prowess. In fact, there were always academic stars in CC — one of the brothers built a personal computer in his room from scratch, this at about the same time IBM launched the PC and Apple the Macintosh. However, as a group, CC brothers were not exactly pushing up the curve.

Nor was the space conducive for studying. Though most of us had single rooms, as a freshman I was assigned a double with a guy who always had a television on. If that wasn't enough, even with the door closed, we had to manage frequent interruptions, from brothers stopping by to talk about their various exploits, to music being played loud enough to be heard throughout the floor.

My two hours of "studying" for that physical chemistry exam by glancing through the notes in my dorm room with the television blaring in the background and music playing down the hall proved to be a failed experiment. I didn't need another "data point," nor could I afford one. The semester was moving quickly and it would have been futile to try to bounce back from two poor exam grades. The next big exam was in physics.

I resolved to try studying in the Stratton Library, a study space on the fifth floor of the Student Center that was open 24 hours a day. Why I moved my workspace to Stratton was fuzzy. Maybe I was trying to avoid MIT's tradition of showering freshmen in the dorm before the first physics exam, a sort of rite of passage. More likely, I must have known that to garner deep understanding of my courses, I needed a quiet space. After all, I used to get up early to study while I was in high school, particularly during my senior year when I took my hardest courses, though these were relatively easy compared to what I was now encountering in college. It just so happened that mornings in my house were the quietest time, though I thought I was doing it just because of my sleep pattern.

The decision to study in Stratton may have also been influenced by my older brother, Keith, who used to speak about how he used the quiet of Stratton to write his senior thesis. Regardless of my reasoning at the time, I'm glad I made this change. It was the first of several important changes.

## "DEEP DIVE" LEARNING: PREPARING FOR MY FIRST PHYSICS EXAM

I decided to set aside two days — not just two hours — to study before the next exam. Once again, I don't know what prompted that decision, but I must have thought that with an extra day, I'd have a backup evening to study if for whatever reason I *couldn't* begin two days ahead of time. Moreover, a two-day advance would give me time to get any lingering questions answered on the day before the exam.

I committed to reviewing all of the textbook reading and my lecture notes in detail. To go back to the beginning. Much of what is taught in these courses is "vertical"; new material builds on the previous material. I knew that if my foundational knowledge was shaky — and it was — then I would struggle to understand more advanced concepts that were being introduced in a rapid-fire manner. On the other hand, I reasoned, if I can go back to the beginning of the semester and shore up the foundational principles, the rest of the material will come more easily. I resolved not to move to another concept until I deeply understood the previous one, and not just to understand *The What* — that is, the steps I needed to follow to derive an equation or procedure — but most importantly, *The Why*.

During the first afternoon and evening that I set aside, I reviewed the reading material from the textbook and from my lecture notes. I read every page, every word, and worked out every sample problem. I knew I needed to take notes *of* my notes, and I wrote these "notes of notes" in a separate notebook that I dedicated for this purpose. (Today, students would probably use an iPad handwriting app like *Noteshelf* or *OneNote*.) I knew from high school that I best remembered new material when I wrote it down, especially if I wrote the concepts, facts, definitions, or procedures in my own words.

Mine was an active review — reading, writing, highlighting, and noting questions in the margins of the notebook. If I didn't understand a word, phrase, procedure, or step, or I thought it was a concept or definition I needed to remember, I wrote it down in the dedicated notebook.

I didn't realize it at the time, but this notebook would prove helpful in preparing me for the final exam later in the semester because the exam schedule did not lend itself to the "deep dive" I was now undertaking. Some colleges have a two-week reading period that allows sufficient time for students to review a semester's worth of material. At MIT at the time, classes ended on a Friday, and exams — which could occur on three consecutive days — began the following Monday. Not much time to study at all!

## TWO-HOUR BLOCKS, THEN SHORT BREAKS

In preparing for this physics test, I would work for two hours straight and then take a break by walking around the library or using the restroom. Occasionally I would go down to the coffee shop two floors below to grab a cup or some other snack to keep me energized. On a few occasions, I would venture into the arcade. I wasn't a big video gamer at the time, but I would enjoy watching others play. Strange, I know. It may have been because I didn't have much money as a student. Whatever the reason, I was fortunate never to have been caught up in the video-game vortex. Watching one or two games would be enough of a break for me. I had work to do and I was eager to get back to it.

I stayed in the library well past midnight until I had completed the review. I recall feeling a growing sense of accomplishment. I was finally getting it. More importantly, I was struck by the contrast between how foreign the material felt when I heard or saw it in lecture for the first time, and now weeks later how familiar it became going back and reading for understanding. The subject matter that had seemed to be composed of random and long derivations and diagrams began to make sense to me. Now I needed to figure out how to close that knowledge gap in the future, and in my other courses.

The real test, of course, was how I would do on the exam in two days, but the first day of "deep dive" studying boded well for me. I remember thinking, "I may have found my weapon for counterattacking the MIT monster," a weapon I would eventually employ and teach throughout my career.

## ONE DAY TO GO: A RELENTLESS PURSUIT OF MASTERY

The next day — one day before the exam — I sought out my teaching assistant to answer the questions I had uncovered during my "deep dive." I am not an outgoing person, and I typically didn't feel confident reaching out to my professors and TAs, at least until I had something specific to ask. This is one instance when I did. The "deep dive" gave me confidence to ask questions. Preparation produces confidence, even for an introvert like me who tended to be intimidated by the preeminence of these great minds.

The other good news is I had only a few questions, because I had gone through the work so thoroughly.

After classes were over for the day, and once I got my questions answered, I returned to the library. It was still early, with few students there, so I was able to choose the same cubicle. That location had worked for me the night before and it was quickly becoming familiar. I had already discovered the power of context; if there was a place that I could associate with certain activities like studying, then in the future, it would be easier to be motivated to work on that activity simply by showing up in that place. That cubicle in the library became my place for serious study. And while I couldn't always reserve that specific space (after all, there were about 8,000 other students on campus at the time), I discovered that any cubicle in that library produced the same effect on me.

And now, the night before the exam, after understanding *The Why*, the goal was to apply what I had learned: in other words, to work problems. I brought with me old problem sets and their accompanying "solution sets" (the answers that the TAs provided after they returned your graded assignments and exams). I had my dedicated notebook from the previous night's "deep dive," of course, where I'd recorded what I learned and what I didn't understand. I had my textbook and my lecture notes, old problem sets and solution sets, and old exams that upperclassmen in Chocolate City and other living groups maintained in their own notebook "libraries." I brought highlighters. (I even brought mechanical pencils so I wouldn't have to get up to sharpen them.)

And I made sure I had plenty of paper. In the early '80s, computer terminals were accompanied by dot-matrix printers with stacks of connected paper that were fed into the printers. Occasionally, a print job would go awry and someone would discard the printout. I'd grab a stack of the discards because the backside was blank and perfectly usable for scrap.

So I was well equipped for the job ahead.

Again, my focus was on learning the material deeply, and I wasn't going to leave until I understood it. Bringing all of these materials to my study space deprived me of any reason to interrupt my learning. The automaker Lexus has a well-known tag line that speaks to their quality brand: "A Relentless Pursuit of Perfection." I adopted an internal narrative that defined my own work, too: A Relentless Pursuit of Mastery.

I began by reviewing my notes in the dedicated notebook from the previous night's "deep dive." And I reviewed answers to the questions I had posed to the TA earlier in the day — the concepts, procedures or terms I had stumbled over the night before.

I worked problems. I reworked every example in the reading, being careful to understand every explanation. I then moved to my lecture notes, working those problems that were presented in class, making sure I understood every step — again, not just *The What*, but *The Why*.

Next, I worked every problem in the problem sets as if I was seeing it for the first time. Though I had the solution sets — the corrected answers — in hand, I resisted the urge to passively consult the answers. I stayed with a problem until I got it. Only if I got stuck did I pull out the solution set, and then just so I could get insight into the next step — *The Why* as well as *The What* — and the next step only; then I'd put the solutions away to see if I could solve the problems on my own.

It was a slow, methodical process, but fruitful. A step at a time. A problem. A page. A derivation at a time. The Relentless Pursuit of Mastery. I was determined to understand everything. And the conceptual "deep dive" I'd conducted the previous night gave me the intellectual backdrop for this problem-solving session. Attaching theory and practice proved essential for me; it grounded the theory in something I could do and see, and it placed the problems into context.

The last thing I did that night was to see if I could solve the problems on a previous exam as if I were in the test environment. I gave myself the customary 55 minutes, the same amount I would have the next day, and proceeded to attack the work. Once again, when I got stuck, I consulted the solution set, then went back and reworked the problem as if I had not seen the answers. It took longer than the allotted time, but at the end of the evening, I knew the material intimately. I had *mastered* the topics and I was prepared for the physics test.

I returned to the dormitory after the freshman rite-of-passage showers were done. I had missed them…for now. (They caught me later that semester, though.) My classmates and I spoke briefly about the exam and the material, but it was hard to maintain focus in the wake of the showers.

That night, I literally dreamt about free-body-force diagrams—the forces that act on a body of mass. Really! I recall seeing the images of blocks sliding down ramps, with force vectors emanating from the top, front, and back of each block. The material that was going to be tested the next day had become so embedded in my consciousness that I actually dreamt the problems, and the solutions. Neuroscientists have discovered that the brain consolidates its neural connections while we sleep, and moves memories from the short-term to the long-term regions of the brain. (I'll discuss this further in Chapter 4.) I was actually getting smarter as I slept. For me at the time, dreaming of physics was a validation that I had approached the work correctly, and that I knew the content well. I was prepared and confident. Not cocky, just confident, and it showed.

The next day was the first time I walked out of an MIT exam confident that I had aced it. Not only did I know the material, I finished all the problems in sufficient time to review my answers. It turned out that the discipline of working problems — lots of them — the night before had not only increased my understanding, but also the speed at which I solved problems. *I had made myself smarter.*

## "DEEP DIVE" LEARNING: IT WORKED!

The results confirmed it: I earned a grade that was higher than the class average. I was gratified that the strategy worked. Gone would be the days when I would question my abilities. I had found a successful formula, and I made a commitment to stick with it. I began to apply this strategy to all my technical courses: starting my "deep dive" two days before the exam to obtain a conceptual understanding of the topics, to formulate and get answers to questions, and to work through the readings and notes.

It became a formula for success: I graduated with a 4.6/5.0 cumulative grade-point average. To think how far I had come! From a 38 in the first exam of freshman year, to an A/A- GPA over the course of four years. I was the same person I had been when I arrived. The only difference was in how I approached the work.

I made three essential shifts:

- **AN ATTITUDE SHIFT**

I made a commitment that I would be successful. My encounter with Professor Witt was the catalyst. In a strange and blunt way, he reminded me that I could be successful in college, but that I needed a new way of working. I had to make a commitment to learn all of the material, and not just in a cursory fashion. Mastery had to be my goal, not just better grades. I also believed that I *could* get smarter, that my lack of preparation in high school would not relegate me to chronic 38s. This attitude shift was a huge breakthrough.

- ## A CONNECTIONS SHIFT

As a second means of getting to mastery, I also needed to be more committed to reaching out to TAs and professors to get my questions answered. I had to overcome my shyness and introverted tendencies and press forward to get help when I needed it. I had previously regarded the professors and TAs as paragons of thought and intellect. While I didn't think any less of them, I realized that quality informal interactions with them — conversational connections — were as essential to my success as those that took place in more formal settings.

I also had to change the nature of my interactions with the "brothers" of my living group. I loved these guys, but studying had to come first. I knew that in order for me to learn the material, I needed to separate from them until I had a chance to synthesize it; only then could I come back and enjoy their company and benefit from their assistance. My friends could no longer be my lifeboat. I had to power my own boat, and work with them as an equal rather than as an intellectual stowaway.

- ## A BEHAVIOR SHIFT

Finally, I needed a new approach to learning. The *Deep Dive Learning Approach* that I stumbled upon had led to proficiency. It required me to use a different venue — the 24-hour library. And it required me to set aside a specific — and sufficient — time to study: those two full days before each exam, to review everything and to work all the problems.

# NOW IT'S YOUR TURN TO MAKE THE SHIFTS

These are the three strategies I followed that turned my fate around. These three shifts — these Smart Shifts — are the key to working smarter. I've taught them to hundreds of students and parents at MIT and elsewhere, and just as happened to me, I've seen the students who follow them do remarkably better in class, and on their exams. Some are in college today, while others have already gone on to earn PhDs or enter the workforce. Though the technologies we use today such as laptops, tablets and wireless communication are markedly different from the mechanical pencils and discarded mainframe-computer paper that were available during my college days, the principles are timeless. This method works. These three Smart Shifts can help you succeed.

Now it's time to take our own "deep dive" into each of them.

CHAPTER 2

# THE ATTITUDE SHIFT

*"Achievement: Unless you try to do something beyond what you have already mastered, you will never grow."*

*- Ralph Waldo Emerson*

*"The brain rarely gets it right the first time, and making mistakes is key to developing intelligence."*

*- Eric Jensen [1]*

## INTRODUCTION

THE FIRST STEP toward working smarter is to shift your attitude. You may arrive at college having had a great high school experience — at the top of the proverbial totem pole, with a drawer full of academic awards, varsity letters, and community service accolades. Or you may have barely survived high school and are looking for a new beginning in college. If you're in the first group, you expect to carry your high school experience forward; you view college as more of the same — "Grades 13+" — rather than a dramatically new experience. If you're in the second group, then you're looking to make a fresh start. No matter which group you're in, you'll find that college is a very different world.

No longer are there parents or guardians in person to wake you up in the morning, fix breakfast, monitor what you eat, and force you to do homework. Most professors won't spoon-feed information, teach to the middle of the class' level, or slow the pace of the course just to make sure everyone understands the material before moving on to the next topic. In college, you have to step up your game, while you move toward independence as an emerging adult. And though you may not have as structured a day as you did in high school (each period scheduled from 8 a.m. to 3 p.m.), the *pace* of life in college — both academic and social — is typically much faster.

## COLLEGE CHALLENGES YOUR SENSE OF SMARTNESS

Many of you have been considered smart all your life. And you've had sufficient success to "prove" the label. After all, your grades were good. You were in the top half of your class. You didn't have to work as hard as the next guy or gal. Rarely did you have to ask for help with your schoolwork or to understand a concept or topic. Your fellow students came to *you* to ask for help. You may even have been recognized for your academic accomplishments. You got what was going on, and you may have gotten it quickly. Clearly, you were a star.

If you weren't in the top half of your high school class, by contrast, you may have graduated with a sense of accomplishment that was born out of struggle. You may have been temporarily satisfied that you'd earned a diploma, but the hard-fought success may have left you with lingering doubts about whether or how you'd be successful in college.

In college, either the tables are turned (if you were one of the stars), or they confirm what you suspected (if you were one of the strugglers.) You *think* you work hard, but you don't immediately see the results commensurate with your effort. And slowly, you may begin to doubt yourself. You eventually find yourself in a position where you wonder if everyone is smarter than you. Others seem to know all the answers, or can engage in a classroom discussion before you can even ask a question. Like television programs after a football game that goes into overtime, you may feel at times that you've joined a class "already in progress."

It can feel that way. *But that doesn't make it true.*

Most students believe that "the smart ones" never have the crisis of confidence I've just described. Even more dangerously, they believe that if they themselves are going through that sort of crisis, then they must not be among "the smart ones." In reality, though, most students — no matter which group they were in during high school — experience the very same feelings you're feeling. What matters at this juncture — what separates the mediocre college student from the excellent one — is how they respond.

## YOUR ATTITUDE DETERMINES YOUR ALTITUDE

It was the great motivational speaker, Zig Ziglar, who said, "Your attitude, not your aptitude, will determine your altitude." I don't *wholly* agree with him; I do think that aptitude has something to do with your success. But I believe that it plays a different role in the success equation: Your attitude *precedes* your aptitude. **In other words, you can become smarter by applying yourself in a certain way.**

So I would modify Mr. Ziglar's quote this way: "Your attitude influences your aptitude. *Together,* they determine your altitude." Still, his point is well taken. In my years as a college administrator, I noticed that the students who ultimately do well in school react in a different way to the crisis of confidence than the students who ultimately do poorly or get stuck at a level of mediocrity. Those top students realize that the approach they used in high school is no longer working for them, and they *decide* to change their approach. They're not afraid to learn from the best, to ask questions, or to model their behavior after those who were excelling. Their mindset says, "I must get better, and I will."

The other student also makes a decision, but this decision is more likely to be fatal to his chance of college success: Rather than partnering with someone who is doing well — because doing so would be considered an indictment of his own abilities — he prefers to link up with others who are also struggling. (I use "he" here deliberately, because while both male and female students can behave this way, it's far more

common among the guys.) These new friends coalesce around low expectations and low performance. They celebrate mediocrity, and poor
grades become a point of celebration, rather than a point of shame and
a spur to greater efforts. The posse masks their own sense of self-doubt.

Is there another way — a better way — to deal with that doubt?
Absolutely.

## OVERCOMING AN INFERIORITY COMPLEX

It's no surprise that some students feel inferior when they get to college. Invariably, you meet students who had a more rigorous high
school background; they may have traveled more extensively than you;
or come from a family earning more (and in some cases much more)
than your family. Compared to the struggles that you're experiencing,
these students appear to be gliding through their first years of college.
Over time, your feelings of inferiority can lead to serious self-doubt:
even to an inferiority complex where, psychologists say, you internalize your supposed shortcomings. You can become so discouraged with
yourself and your capabilities that you "shrink back" from taking on
difficult tasks. A self-defeating attitude then creates a self-fulfilling
prophecy.

I struggled with this during my freshman year. My roommate was
private school-educated and had a strong background in chemistry and
literature. I, on the other hand, went to public schools (albeit a magnet
high school), but never had chemistry or biology, and had never been
called upon to write a paper longer than a few pages. Everything seemed
to come easily for him, and so he spent a fair amount of time watching
television in our shared room.

Imagine my surprise when I finally realized that he had an inferiority complex, too! His early months in college had been so easy
because he had covered the material in high school, and so he slacked
off. When new material came along, he struggled — a totally new experience for him. He was one of those students who had always equated

his success with his smartness. When he no longer had success, rather than decoupling the two and trying to figure out a new strategy, he instead retreated from his schoolwork and started to unravel academically. Meanwhile, I learned how to plod along, daily, consistently, in a focused approach that ultimately helped me overcome my lack of confidence and succeed.

We both suffered from an inferiority complex — the difference was in how we responded to it. One of us let negative feelings take control. And one of us found a new way to get through it.

If you are suffering from an inferiority complex, take heart. The advice I'm about to give you in this chapter will put you on path to avoid that crippling negativism.

## DEFENSIVE PESSIMISM

One outgrowth of an inferiority complex, I've found, is what researchers call "defensive pessimism."

That's the attitude where academically insecure students — Black and Latino students especially, but also women in certain settings — set low expectations at the start of a challenging class. "The best I'll do in this class is a 'C,'" they tell themselves. University of Wisconsin researchers Aaron Brower and Annmarie Ketterhagen, who uncovered this phenomenon, suspect that defensive pessimism is a way to mentally protect students against failure if they experience it, even if they secretly hope and expect to do better. But they also suggest that it's a counterintuitive way to get motivated.

White male students in this same study, by contrast, adopted a totally opposite attitude. They employed "strategic optimism." In other words, they set high expectations, and they'd feel satisfied only if they scored within a half a grade below the high bar they'd set for themselves, or even better.

If you find yourself making low-ball pronouncements about your anticipated performance in a class or on a test, then you're suffering from "defensive pessimism." It's an attitudinal disease. You have to shift your attitude.

Of course, you can also go too far.

## OVERCOMING DELUSIONAL THINKING

There's a difference between "strategic optimism" and outright delusion. The latter can be every bit as damaging as its inferiority-complex partner at the opposite end of the spectrum. These delusional types are the ones who think more highly of themselves than they ought. They go about believing that they're smarter and more influential than they actually are. These students, says researcher William Sedlacek, fail to make a realistic self-appraisal — which also can undermine their ability to change course when it becomes necessary.

This kind of thinking can afflict corporations as well as individuals. When I was in college, two companies, the Boston-based Digital Equipment Corporation (DEC) and Rochester, New York-based Kodak, were leaders in their industries for a period of time, but they suffered from the same delusional thought process. When the market changed — personal computers in the case of DEC, and digital photography for Kodak — they failed to adapt and respond to these changes quickly enough to retain their leadership position, and both lost market share to more agile and self-aware rivals.

Like these two corporate giants, "delusional" students come into college as academic behemoths, thinking they're better than others. They may be children of wealth, or of a private school education. They may have been the valedictorian of their high school. And they've never really experienced academic failure, the way I did on my first physical chemistry exam. Suddenly, they have an experience in college that challenges their self-beliefs. However, because of their delusional thinking, they don't admit (at least publicly) to being in trouble or needing help. Like DEC and Kodak, they don't admit to the changing landscape and ultimately are left behind.

When I was a dean, I had a freshman advisee who was very delusional in his thinking. He arrived in college having all of the privileges afforded to him — a rigorous high school education, the most popular brand of clothing, etc. He had an elitist attitude, even toward other African Americans: He was too good for them. He eventually got through freshman year, but only after surviving a semester of academic probation when he finally humbled himself, heeded advice from me and from others, and realized he needed help. The story ends well; he eventually graduated from the university. But it was a close call. It could have gone much more smoothly for him if he hadn't arrived at college with such a high-brow attitude, or if he'd been more willing to re-examine that attitude when he faced new circumstances.

Because you can't change your approach until you've changed your attitude.

## WHY ATTITUDE MATTERS

You rarely *do* something unless you *decide* to do it. Other than breathing, blinking, digesting food, or reacting to danger, we human beings exercise decision-making control over most of our functions. Before we invest in an effort or in an activity, we *decide* to do it. Accordingly, you must *decide* to get better before you *do* get better. In fact, you must have already decided to get better, because you chose to read this book!

No quote captures the essence of what I believe on this subject better than William James, who said, "It is our attitude at the beginning of a difficult task which, more than anything else, will affect its successful outcome." Your attitude precedes your actions, which in turn affect what you accomplish. Albert Bandura, who has published volumes of studies on confidence and motivation, says it this way: "What people think, believe, and feel affects how they behave." If you can align your attitude, you can get your behavior in line as well. That's why we begin with the "Attitude Shift."

Your beliefs — your attitude — are linked with the goals you set, and your motivation to achieve those goals. If you believe you're going to be successful, you're more likely to set ambitious goals and then put forth the effort to achieve them. On the other hand, if you have a self-defeating attitude, you'll probably set low goals — or even no goals — so you won't feel bad about yourself for not achieving them. You certainly won't feel *motivated* to achieve them.

Back to William James' quote: "It is our attitude at the beginning of a difficult task which, more than anything else, will affect its successful outcome."

So what can affect your attitude? Or to put it more practically, how can *you* affect your attitude? How can you improve your chances for a "successful outcome"?

It may all boil down to a question of Mindset. Or actually, two questions:

- How do you view your own intelligence?
- What's your level of confidence?

Your answers to those two questions, it shouldn't surprise you to learn, are tightly connected. Let's see how.

## THE FIXED MINDSET VS. THE GROWTH MINDSET

How you view your intelligence, it turns out, has a bearing on how you respond when you feel challenged. Researcher Carol Dweck has coined the term "Mindset" to distinguish between those individuals who view their intelligence as unchangeable — the "fixed mindset" — versus those who view their intelligence as expandable — the "growth mindset." The fixed- mindset person believes that everyone is born with a fixed amount of intelligence, and that each person's intel-ligence occupies a permanent position along an intelligence bell curve. These poor souls at the low end of the curve (according to fixed-mindset people) are not only born there; they're destined to stay there. They're relegated to a life of low-quality schools, menial jobs, ghetto housing, etc.

By contrast — or so the fixed-mindset theory would have you believe — are the select few located on the right-hand side of the curve, at the upper levels of intelligence. These are the so-called geniuses, blessed with high IQs and entitled to all the privileges that supposedly go with that status: better schools, better jobs, nicer neighborhoods, and more attractive spouses and children.

This fixed-mindset belief is so deeply embedded in society that many of us often appraise our own performances — on standardized tests, high school rankings, and what colleges we attend — based on where we think we fall along this distribution curve. In fact, when teachers and professors return our exams and papers, we have a natural tendency to locate ourselves — and lock ourselves in — somewhere along that curve. (And the teachers may have done it to us, too.)

As the label suggests, fixed-mindset people believe that one's intelligence can't be changed; their intelligence is as core to their being as their DNA or skin color. These people might concede that a person can learn some new things — gain more knowledge — but that how any individual brain fundamentally operates, its critical thinking and the speed with which it reasons and solves problems, is unchangeable.

There are a number of unfortunate side effects to this fixed mindset.

**First, fixed-mindset people seem to thrive only when they have confidence that a task is already within their grasp.** They will not take on too big a challenge if it means their own beliefs about their intelligence would be called into question. If the work becomes too challenging, they're more likely to become frustrated or simply lose interest. As a professor, Dr. Dweck saw this happen among pre-med students in their first-semester chemistry class. If they did well right away, then they retained their interest. However, those fixed-mindset students who struggled lost their love of chemistry. One student wrote, "The harder it gets, the more I have to force myself to read the book and study for the tests. I was excited about chemistry before, but now every time I think about it, I get a bad feeling in my stomach.'"[2]

**Second, fixed-mindset people feel smart only when their work is flawless — and it's hard to be flawless.** When asked about when they felt smart, fixed-mindset people (children as well as adults) responded, "It's when I don't make mistakes." "When I finish something fast and it's perfect." "When something is easy for me, but other people can't do it."[3] For those who are of this mindset, any failure, even making a simple mistake, is an indictment of their ability. Repeated failure, meanwhile, is tragic. As one writer put it, in the minds of these people, "failure is transformed from an action ('I failed') to an identity ('I am a failure')."[4]

**Third, fixed-mindset people believe that effort is a threat to their identity — and learning often requires effort.** Their take, according to Dweck: Effort is for those who don't have ability. They believe that if you're really smart, then work should come easily to you. If you have to work hard — like I did in college — then you must not be smart.

**Finally, fixed-mindset people, already struggling with questions about belonging, are more susceptible to prevailing stereotypes — and stereotypes hold them back even further.** In one of Dweck's studies, college women who were interested in math-related disciplines and were currently taking a math course were asked to report their feelings about math and their sense of belonging. Specifically, she asked them if they felt like a "full-fledged member of the math community" or like "an outsider." Did they feel "comfortable" or did they feel "anxious"? Did they feel good or bad about their math skills?[5] Fixed-mindset thinkers, she found, "felt a shrinking sense of belonging" as the semester went on. "And the more they felt the presence of stereotyping in their class, the more their comfort with math withered…The stereotyping of low ability was able to invade them — to define them — and take away their comfort and confidence."[6]

## THE MINDSETS IN ACTION

Let's dig a little deeper into these two types of students: the fixed-mindset students who often fail to respond to academic challenges, and the growth-mindset students who view those same challenges as opportunities to change their approach to learning.

The former, as we've seen, are afraid that any negative experience undermines what they've always believed about themselves, that they were successful because they were smart. The link between success and smartness is hard-coded in their minds, so even a temporary setback raises disconcerting questions about their underlying intelligence.

These fixed-mindset students, faced with a crisis of confidence, begin to get discouraged and choose not to figure out how to get better or smarter; doing so might subject them to even more of those disconcerting questions. So they withdraw, or act out, or simply divert their attention to other pursuits like their jobs, or their music, or — like my freshman roommate did — simply watching television. At least that way they can explain away their lack of performance by suggesting they're not working that many hours. The alternative story line is very uncomfortable for them. Their great fear, according to Dweck, is having to admit, "I gave it my all and it wasn't good enough."

Fortunately, there's another approach — another group. *A group you can join.*

The growth-mindset student believes that intelligence is not fixed, but that it's malleable, and expandable. These students believe that their intelligence is something that can be developed. They believe that they *can* become smarter by applying themselves and by tackling situations that will *make* them smarter. They seek out challenges. They embrace effort as a route to intellectual development and subject mastery. They know that mastery, and not just getting good grades, is the goal.

When these students were asked about when *they* feel smart, their answers provided quite a contrast to those in the fixed-mindset group. Growth-mindset students responded, "When it's really hard, and I try really hard, and I can do something I couldn't do before," or "[When] I work on something a long time and I start to figure it out."

A very telling long-term study of UC Berkeley students discovered that growth-mindset students gain confidence when they repeatedly met and succeeded at challenges. This suggests that a growth-mindset and confidence are linked — that the process is self-reinforcing. That makes sense, doesn't it? If you believe you can get better or smarter, you're more likely to embrace new challenges with confidence, and focus more effort on the task at hand, even a difficult task. Growth-mindset individuals stick longer with difficult problems. They're more likely to bounce back when they suffer setbacks, and they experience less anxiety around tests or other performance assessments.

"The passion for stretching yourself and sticking to it, even (or especially) when it's not going well, is the hallmark of the growth mindset," Dweck explains. "This is the mindset that allows people to thrive during some of the most challenging times in their lives."

Remember those psyched-out pre-med students I mentioned earlier? If they'd been growth minded, they wouldn't have lost interest in chemistry. Instead, they would have viewed the challenging first-semester chemistry course as an opportunity to adjust their study habits. They also would have been motivated by the fact that chemistry, along with biology, form the basis for most medical science — another reason to try to master the material. By embracing challenges, and sometimes having success in overcoming them, you gain confidence in your ability to perform. There is nothing more satisfying than working on something for a while and having the pieces fall into place.

"I start to figure it out."

So can you.

## EMBRACE EFFORT

The reform-minded sharks in Disney's animated movie *Finding Nemo* had a memorable line: "Fish are friends, not food." I'd make a similar point about effort. "Effort is a friend, not an enemy." Growth-mindset people embrace effort as a means to learning and mastery. Growth-mindset people thrive when they embrace challenge, and when they begin to understand or do something they couldn't do before. They aren't ashamed to ask questions, seek out help, or otherwise "look dumb," because they keep the big picture in mind: Mastery. They realize that theirs is a *process* toward proficiency, and not just about looking good or *feeling* smart. While fixed-mindset types see effort as an unwelcome reminder of their "deficiencies," growth-minded thinkers know that it sometimes takes prodigious, concentrated effort to get there — effort that has the power to transform them as a person.

So let me ask you: Which mindset is more likely to lead to success?

## EMBRACE MISTAKES: ARE YOU READY TO FAIL?

When my youngest son was learning how to ride a bicycle without training wheels, I asked him if he was willing to fall. He said he wasn't. I told him that I wouldn't teach him to ride until he was. After two days of this back-and-forth dialogue, he finally saw my point and grudgingly told me that he was willing to fall. (He did, however, put on knee pads, gloves, a helmet, and elbow pads before getting on the bike. "Smart" kid!) You can't expect to learn unless you're willing to risk failure.

Growth-mindset students don't mind making mistakes. As my good friend Dr. Jeff Howard, founder of the Boston-based Efficacy Institute, states, mistakes (or any performance, for that matter) are simply "data" that people with growth mindsets use to shape more effective strategies going forward. Missing a field goal doesn't — or at least shouldn't — cause a kicker to avoid high-pressure situations. Rather, the growth-minded kicker watches videotape to find out what he did wrong, and then works with the holder to improve his approach to the next kick.

Similarly, my infamous 38 in physical chemistry was simply data, not an indictment — data that I used to develop the new approach to learning that I'm sharing with you.

I met Dr. Howard when I was a senior in college. He and his team introduced me to the growth mindset when I was contemplating running for Vice Chairperson of a national student organization, (coincidentally the one for which I work today). His workshop challenged me to question why I was running for Vice Chair, and not for Chair, a position that was also open. I was confronted with the reality that fear dictated my decision: defensive pessimism in action! Fear of failure. Fear of putting myself out there. Wondering if anyone could move from Vice President of a local student chapter to National Chair without traversing the customary interim steps, such as chapter presidency or regional leadership. That was fixed-mindset thinking.

Instead, Jeff's workshop challenged me to wonder what I had to lose by aiming higher. I would learn an enormous amount about myself as a candidate, and about the electoral process — submitting paperwork, preparing and giving speeches, giving interviews, etc., even if I lost. I would get exposed to a broader group of people if I aimed for the top spot instead of settling for second fiddle.

That weekend transformed me from a fixed- to a growth-mindset thinker. Eventually, I won the election as National Chair, and developed many of the skills and contacts that I use today, nearly 30 years later.

## LIBERATED THINKING: THROWING OFF STEREOTYPES

A growth mindset is liberating. It frees up precious brain matter that would otherwise be dedicated to figuring out what people think of you. Rather than wondering whether people think you're smart enough, you can fully focus on learning the content or performing the job at hand. Remember: Your goal is mastery, not some false and shallow projection of "smartness" or success.

A growth mindset also frees you from being stereotyped, and even from the threat of it. Researcher Claude Steele of Stanford University and his colleagues found that when students care about something, but are subject to a negative group stereotype in that task or situation — then they'll actually perform more poorly than they would if that "stereotype threat" were lifted or non-existent. For instance, he found that if you told Black students that a test would evaluate their intellectual ability *compared to other students (including non-Blacks)*, they would do more poorly on the test than if they were told that the test would simply be self-diagnostic. In other words, for some students of color, telling them that their intellectual ability would be compared to other (non-Black) students triggers a self-defeating stereotype about intellectual inferiority, leading to lower performance.

Dr. Steele and others have found this same "stereotype threat" among women when they're challenged on their math ability, and among white males on their athletic prowess. The bottom line is this: **You are not at your best when you are experiencing emotional or identity stress.**

Growth-mindset individuals, you won't be surprised to hear, are less likely to get tangled in this stereotype threat. Going back to those female math majors, Dr. Dweck discovered that despite the stereotyping (e.g., professors who exclaimed that their correct answer to a question was a "good guess"), the growth-minded female students continued to feel a part of the math program; they remained confident in their abilities and resolute about their major.

> One student described it this way. "In a math class, [female] students were told they were wrong when they were not (they were in fact doing things in novel ways). It was absurd, and reflected poorly on the instructor not to 'see' the students' good reasoning. It was alright because we were working in groups and we were able to give and receive support among us students...We discussed our interesting ideas among ourselves."[7]

It was their attitude that pulled them through. In the midst of a potentially challenging environment, they adopted new strategies that helped them maintain their interest and continue to thrive.

# YOU CAN CHANGE! (THE SCIENCE SAYS SO!)

Neuroscientists have more recently discovered that there's a biological link to this positive, growth mindset. In fact, these scientists have discovered that our brains have the ability to reorganize themselves by forming new neural connections in response to new situations or environmental changes. They refer to this remapping as "neuroplasticity." This phenomenon has challenged the prevailing norm of most of the 20th century that our brains, and intelligence, become fixed traits after a critical period during early childhood. Now, thanks to this new line of study, researchers have discovered that our brains remain "plastic" well into adulthood. They discovered this phenomenon in patients who lose a portion of the brain in an accident or because of disease but who, after specific and targeted stimulation, begin to recover some brain function as the healthy portion of the brain takes over functions lost by the damaged parts. The brain does this by forming new neural connections that are stimulated by activity.

Connections between brain cells — neurons — are the basis for learning and memory. Our brains have billions of cells and billions of neural connections. When a new idea, thought, or memory is formed, it is formed because our neurons are making connections.

By applying yourself to a new and challenging task, you're actually stimulating new neural connections. As you start to "figure it out", those connections are reinforced. The next time you're faced with a similar problem, you'll remember what to do. Repetition then solidifies those connections so much so that — and this might seem counterintuitive — you don't have to think about it anymore. It comes "naturally." Consider anything you do now — typing, reading, simple multiplication, driving — that you don't have to think much about compared to the first time you did it. With repetition, your brain gets more efficient; it prunes away unused connections and optimizes the necessary functions. That's how I got so good at solving problems: because the day before an exam I would spend hours simply *working problems*. I developed a problem-solving rhythm that not only increased my understanding of the concepts, but enabled me to finish my exams with enough time to go back to check my work. A double win.

## SO WHAT ABOUT YOU?

Dr. Dweck closes her opening chapter on *Mindset* with a series of questions. Let me set them out as a checklist — and a challenge — to you:

> Is there something in your past that you think measured you? A test score? A dishonest or callous action? Being fired from a job? Being rejected? Focus on that thing. Feel all of the emotions that go with it. Now put it in a growth-mindset perspective. Look honestly at your role in it, but understand it doesn't define your intelligence or personality. Instead, ask: What did I (or can I) learn from that experience? How can I use it as a basis for growth? Carry that with you instead."[8]

Why does this matter? Remember that creative license I applied to Zig Ziglar's quote? "Your attitude influences your aptitude. *Together,* they determine your altitude." At the end of the day, achievement matters, and growth leads the way to achievement, whatever your desired outcome may be: mastery of some particular subject matter, or better grades, or higher overall satisfaction in college or in the workplace.

Let me cite one final study that Dr. Dweck mentions. When a group of college students were asked to write letters to elementary students about the growth mindset — about the fact that intelligence is malleable — these letter-writing students ended up earning better grades that semester than a similar group that was asked to write to elementary schoolers about the fixed mindset! It's just one more way the growth mindset leads to deeper learning, greater intellectual satisfaction, and better grades.

So: Try adopting your own growth mindset. Make a decision to approach every task and every situation with the belief that everything is possible. That haunting question about whether or not you're smart enough? Take it off the table. You *are* smart — and you can become smarter.

## WORKING SMARTER TAKEAWAYS: THE ATTITUDE SHIFT

- Don't be surprised when college challenges your sense of smartness. What matters is how you respond to the challenge.
- Attitude matters: Before you learn *how to* work smarter, you have to decide that you *want to* work smarter.
- Intelligence is expandable; it can be developed.
- Your attitude precedes your aptitude. You can get smarter by applying yourself.
- Adopt the growth mindset: "I must get better and I will."
- If you feel inferior, don't shrink back, buckle down!
- Never be overconfident; college will humble you. What matters is making a realistic self-appraisal.
- Embrace effort: It'll make you smarter and build confidence.
- Consider mistakes and setbacks as information to learn from, rather than indictments of your ability.
- You'll never learn to ride unless you're willing to fall.
- Never say "I'm not good at it." Instead, say "I'm not good at it — YET."

CHAPTER 3

# THE CONNECTIONS SHIFT

## INTRODUCTION

SOME YEARS AFTER I graduated from college, my good friend Dr. Donna O. Mackey invited me to a workshop she was conducting. Donna and I had served together, when we were both in college, on the executive board of a national organization for engineering students. I was National Chairperson — my candidate sights raised, you'll recall, after participating in that Efficacy workshop — and she was National Vice Chairperson after a very successful tenure as chairperson of her region.

At the point when she extended the invitation, Donna was a practicing chemical engineer and had developed a novel learning approach that if followed precisely, she contended, guaranteed straight "A"s. She wrote a book with much the same title. The *Guaranteed 4.0* system is widely acclaimed and well known, particularly among progressive engineering colleges with large minority populations and a proactive student-affairs administration.

While I found that some of her note-taking requirements were onerous for students, many of the strategies she discussed during the workshop were extremely worthwhile. One step in particular was a recommendation to visit your professor during his or her office hours at least once per week.

As she made this suggestion, I had two immediate reactions. The first was a deep-seated, visceral one. The thought of going to see a professor on a one-on-one (or even a one-on-several) basis had struck fear in me as a student, and it still didn't sit especially well with me as an adult. You see, I'm an introvert by nature, one who draws energy from being alone, as introverts often do. When we're in groups, introverts can be gregarious and engaging, as I had learned to be, but social interactions drain us.

Our characteristics are the polar opposites of those of extroverts, who are energized by social interactions. Not only is my default preference being alone, but the thought of going to see a professor raised my anxiety level (at least momentarily) during Donna's workshop, even though I had frequently worked side-by-side with faculty as a college administrator. My reaction to her admonition surprised me; it resembled the emotional response of an adult whose memory of a childhood trauma has suddenly been triggered.

After I got over that initial reaction, my second thought was to reflect on how often I — as a student — had intentionally gone to see a professor. Not very often. But I recalled that the few occasions during my undergraduate years (many more times in graduate school) were for courses in which I did remarkably well. Was it a coincidence that the classes I thoroughly enjoyed and in which I did well were also those in which I also got to know the professor well?

I remember, for instance, my large multivariable-calculus class during the second semester of my freshman year. My professor, Dr. Ted Shifrin, was also my recitation instructor, so I got to see him five days a week (three days for lecture, and two for recitation). He saw promise in me and suggested that I consider majoring in mathematics. What an endorsement! I felt I could do no wrong in that class, and indeed I did extremely well there. When I reflect on that class even 30-plus years later, I have warm thoughts about it, not just because I enjoyed the subject, but because of the special relationship I had with the professor.

It's worth making the effort to build relationships with professors. But those aren't the only relationships worth building.

Think horizontal. Think vertical.

This chapter makes the case for the power of the connections you need to make in college to be successful. The various strategies I'll share here are based on the work of researcher and author Dr. Vincent Tinto, who argues that the likelihood of a student finishing a degree in college depends on two things: the quality of the relationships with faculty and administration, what I call *vertical integration*; and the quality of the interactions with peers, or *horizontal integration*.

My relationship with my calculus professor demonstrates vertical integration. He not only offered extra assistance, but I got close enough for him to see and affirm my potential as a student and future academic.

It wasn't until graduate school, years later, that I discovered the advantages of working smarter with my peers — horizontal integration — and the power of a peer network to facilitate deep learning.

I was taking a course in microeconomics during the third semester of my doctoral program when one of my classmates suggested we get together to work on our problem sets. In that class, we had weekly homework assignments, each of which had six or seven problems. The class was well-taught, but the concepts required some reflection and synthesis to be understood. I agreed to join a small study group comprising about six of us. We scheduled 90-minute get-togethers to review the problems two days before the problem sets were due. We were each encouraged to work diligently on our own before coming to the study group, so that we'd each have something to contribute. Our goal for the group was not to *do* the problems, but rather, to agree on the preferred *approach* for solving each of the problems.

So we would debate different approaches or formulas, and eventually come to consensus. If we couldn't reach consensus, one of us would volunteer to reach out to the TA that day or the next before the assignment was due, and then email the correct procedure or approach to the rest of the group. We then worked alone to finish the problem sets based on that shared knowledge.

It worked exquisitely. Not only did we all get very good grades, but most importantly, we gained a deep understanding of the material. Going into class, we were confident and actually looked forward to turning in our homework. That confidence, borne out of preparation and robust discussions, carried over into exams as well. At the time, I thought about how powerful and effective this approach was, and how much more I could have learned as an undergraduate if I had employed this strategy back then — work alone, work together, and work alone.

My study group is just one example of successful horizontal integration, but it can also involve your living group, your extracurricular activities, and more generally, your connection with the campus community.

Dr. Tinto makes a compelling case that these connections — both vertical and horizontal — are the keys to success in college. And these critical relationships represent the second major shift, the *Connections Shift*, that is essential to working smarter. Let's begin by taking a deeper look at how to connect with members of the faculty.

## MAKING THE FACULTY CONNECTIONS

*Having faculty members who are perceived by students as being approachable and have high standards and expectations is associated with greater learning.*[9]

In my own research, I discovered that students who were most confident in their academic ability also had strong relationships with faculty. It makes sense that there is a connection between the two, academic confidence and engagement with faculty. Faculty provide students with an important source of confidence through their verbal assessment of your abilities, good or bad. Hearing an affirming statement about your abilities from a faculty member boosts your confidence, and makes you want to work harder in the class. (As with the encouragement I received from Dr. Shifrin, my calculus professor — I didn't want to let him down.) By building strong relationships with faculty outside of class, you increase the likelihood that those encouraging interactions will occur.

But the correlation I discovered between faculty engagement and confidence can work in the other direction as well. If you are more confident in your ability, you are more likely to ask questions in class or otherwise just approach your professor. If you're not confident, your natural tendency — unless you're confronted like I was in the hallway by Professor Witt — is to avoid the professor at all costs. That's understandable, because most students are intimidated by teachers, at least at first. So the key is to drum up enough confidence to approach your professor that first time. If the interaction goes well, and it usually does, it makes the second and subsequent approaches much easier.

And once you've done that, over time you can develop a professional relationship with someone who will appreciate your curiosity and reward you with extra readings, research and internship opportunities, or just the benefit of the doubt if you end up on "the bubble" between an A or a B on a test or a paper. An economics professor during my junior year suggested I apply for the Marshall Scholarship (and that's only because the deadline had already passed for the even more prestigious Rhodes Scholarship.) Sometimes, a professor may see himself or herself in you and decide to invest the time in mentoring you.

The key here is that there is a proven link between faculty engagement and academic self-confidence. You should take advantage of it. Always, in every course. Harvard Kennedy School Professor Richard Light instructs his freshman advisees that they should develop strong relationships with at least one professor each semester, a relationship deep enough so that he or she could write the student a detailed and informative recommendation. Follow Professor Light's advice, and by the time you graduate you'll have at least eight faculty members able to write you a strong recommendation, whether for grad school or for a full-time job. And if you make it only halfway to Professor Light's goal, then you still have four faculty members who know you well, and you've ensured yourself a far richer college experience.

So, how do you engage faculty? I answer this question as the introverted person I introduced you to earlier. I recognize that for many of you, approaching faculty members doesn't come easily. Believe me, I've been there. Let me suggest some ways to gradually leave those feelings behind.

## VISIT EARLY, VISIT OFTEN

When you receive a syllabus for a course, you typically also get a schedule of the professor's office hours. Take advantage of those office hours, preferably during the first two weeks of class: Stop by for a visit. But what if the office hours conflict with your class schedule? Are you out of luck? Not at all. Most professors will happily accommodate a student who wants to see them, even if it's outside their normal office hours, so suggest a time that works for you. Either way, you'll meet the professor during the lowest period of stress for both of you — early in the semester. You don't have to worry about the professor judging you based on your performance in the class because there haven't been assignments due, and you haven't taken exams yet. And, most importantly, professors want to make a good first impression on you and your fellow students, too, so they're typically on their best behavior, the occasional curmudgeon aside. (Some professors just don't care *what* impression they make!)

Go in with a set of questions already in mind, because you may only have 15 minutes. I've suggested that my students ask questions designed to get an overview of the class. In skiing, you learn that you'll go where you're looking. That's why the ski instructor tells the students not to look at the tree... In college, it's equally important to get a big-picture sense of what the course is all about so you'll know where the class is going, and you can anticipate that progression throughout the course.

I would ask your professor these questions:

- "Can you give me an overview of the major topics to be covered this semester?" You would have done your research, of course, by first reviewing the syllabus. You may want to prepare a specific question about one or more of these topics. It might also be a good idea to express particular interest in one of the topics: "I am especially looking forward to when we cover x." And if you're especially bold...

- "Why did you select these topics for our class? Do they align with your research interests?" (And with your own?) And of course, there's one very practical question that's always appropriate:
- "How can I maximize my learning in this class?" Then listen carefully to the details of the answer! They can give you a real head start on succeeding in the class — not to mention a leg up on the competition: those students who couldn't be bothered to schedule such a meeting.

I also recommend you ask about your professor's expectations of you:

- "What kind of work is expected to get an A in the course?"
- "How engaged do you expect students to be in lecture?"
- "Do you accept questions in lecture, or just recitation?"

Finally, since this is a get-to-know-you session, try to make a personal connection, in addition to an intellectual connection. You might have found something in your professor's background that parallels yours. (Again, do your research beforehand.) You may have a hometown in common, or you may share a hobby. Whatever it is that links you, try to highlight that, either as you're opening or you're closing the conversation. Especially if the class is large, the professor is more likely to remember you if you make that connection — but it's good advice regardless of the size of the class. You want the professor to know you by name.

Finally, I like Dr. Mackey's suggestion to go meet with the professor every week. The professor's official office hours are the best times to do so, but as I've already suggested, it's OK to be flexible. Be sure to write each scheduled meeting into your planner (we'll get to that later) and plan to go as if it were a class, even if you don't have a pressing question to ask. Remember, not only are you developing mastery in the course, you're building a relationship.

## GO WITH A FRIEND

You may be enormously shy, or even intimidated at the thought of going to see a professor. No problem: Bring a friend along. There's an old saying in the Bible: "Two are better than one, because they have a good return for their work."[10] You know full well that you take more risks when you have a friend than you would if you were alone. That's human nature. You're bolder, and more willing to face down your fears, when you have someone by your side; there's someone there to back you up, or at least share the experience with you. So don't let your nerves stand in your way — grab a friend in the class and go see the professor together. Make this *vertical* Connections Shift, and you won't miss out on a rich — and potentially rewarding — academic and professional experience.

## USE "BOARD TIME"

My professors used to come into classroom and erase the boards before class. I remember seeing students approach the professor to ask a question or two while the board was being wiped. (In other classes, or in other universities, this ritual might occur after class. Some departments, for instance, insist that the professor who's leaving make the room clean for the prof who follows.) Whether it happens before or after class, while students are filing in or out of the classroom, that "board time" can be a highly valuable time for you.

I recommend that students use "board time" to ask a quick, clarifying question. If it's before class, come with the question already prepared, after you've taken the time to review your notes. It may be something left unclear from previous classes. It may be a question your study group had. This is no time to get into a long discussion, because the professor is getting ready, mentally and logistically, for class. But a brief conversation generally won't interfere with that preparation; the professor may even welcome your question as an indication that further explanation is necessary for previously-taught material.

And of course, if this exchange happens after class, you might focus on something that arose during the class that just ended. Again, it should be something that lends itself to a quick answer. Either way, your question will help you on three fronts. First, it obviously will clarify a concept or idea in your mind. Second, it will help to strengthen your relationship and make you stand out. And finally, as we mentioned a moment ago, it may benefit the class as a whole. If it's a good question, particularly if it's one he or she has received multiple times, the professor may use the first moments of an upcoming class to review or even re-teach the subject. And that second time around may reinforce everyone's understanding — yours and your classmates'.

The takeaway? Use "board time" to strengthen your connections and deepen your knowledge — but use it sparingly. Some professors will welcome the exchange; a few may not. But you'll never know until you try!

## Go to All Exam Reviews

Here's another (strong) suggestion: Never miss an exam review that's taught by your professor and TA. These typically occur a day or two prior to a major exam, during which the professor will review the material that may be tested. This is another touch point for building connections with faculty. While I encourage students to come prepared to ask a few questions after they've done their "deep dive" review, go anyway, whether or not you're prepared. Even if you don't open your mouth, professors will interpret your presence as evidence of your motivation and eagerness to learn, a favorable impression that will serve you well in forging a relationship.

## Get Involved in Research

If you have an opportunity to work with your professor, or any professor, on a research project, grab it. It's your best opportunity to build that strong bond you're seeking. You'll be connecting on an intellectual level in a domain that is near and dear to that professor.

Some colleges may offer opportunities to conduct research for pay, particularly if the professor has grant money available to pay students, or if the university supplements their grant money to bring undergraduates into the research environment. Other institutions may offer research for academic credit. Still others offer neither money nor credit, but may simply encourage students to work with faculty on projects of mutual interest. Whatever the arrangement, working alongside a faculty member on a research project is a huge catalyst for making the Connections Shift.

This is, as you may already suspect, another instance when you have to take the initiative. No one is going to hand you this opportunity. So how do you get started? Well, if you come into college with a particular interest (e.g., robotics, music, the classics, or aircraft), then find a professor who is doing something in that field. Or, during your initial meeting with your professor, you may find the explanation of his or her research interests especially appealing to you. Ask her then, or later, if she has a need for an undergraduate research assistant. (You'll never know if you don't ask.)

A good friend of mine conducted a survey of students who participated in undergraduate research at our university and discovered that a student made on average three requests before securing a research project. So be prepared to get rejected the first or second time, but go in with the attitude that each rejection is a step toward getting what you want.

## MAKING THE ADMINISTRATION CONNECTIONS

Because I was one of those students intimidated by my professors, I relied heavily on several administrators to help me make the vertical part of my Connections Shift. In Chapter 1, I introduced you to my freshman advisor, Dr. Clarence Williams. He was the special assistant to the president of the university, and though I had little contact with the president himself, just knowing that my advisor was so close to the president helped ease my way.

You need a Clarence Williams, someone who knows you by name and can advocate for you if you experience difficulty. More importantly, though, that administrator may prompt you to go see your professor, or introduce you to resources at your school that will help you academically, professionally, or personally. There were others, like Dr. Bill McLaurin, the Director of the Office of Minority Education, who helped me develop and fund a high-school outreach program; and Nels Armstrong, the Associate Director of Admissions, who offered me a job in the Admissions Office and often reminded me that I was admitted on my merit. (His encouraging words were particularly useful when I went through tough patches.)

Later, as a freshman advisor, I would arrange for my advisees to have one-hour roundtables with members of the college's leadership team to demystify "Mahogany Row," where the senior administrative offices were. It also gave these administrators the chance to convey the university's vision, and how to get the most out of the college experience. My advisees met with the president, the provost (who oversees academic affairs such as the faculty), a key dean — the Dean of Engineering, in our case — and others I felt the students should know to help them thrive during their time on campus. My students studied the background of the people they'd be meeting. They'd have studied the organizational chart of the college so they knew the reporting structure. And they'd have prepared questions ahead of time. I also had the young men dress up for the event so they could make a strong visual as well as an intellectual impression. Whenever possible, I'd arrange for the students to meet in the administrator's office or conference room so they could make what is unfamiliar familiar. My purpose, once again: to help them make that vertical Connections Shift by demystifying the institution.

After all, if you know the rules, even the unwritten ones, you're more likely to play well.

But it's not just senior administrators. You should make a point of getting to know the people up and down the organizational chart: in the financial-aid office; the heads of the tutoring service and the writing center; your department chairperson; and all their administrative assistants. Don't ever dismiss this last group as "simply secretaries." In most cases, they are the most knowledgeable about the goings-on in their departments and, if they like you, can easily slot you in for an appointment even if there's officially no room on the calendar. It happens.

## Get to Know Your President

I didn't do this one as an undergrad. I wish I had. You should do it, or at least you should try: Get to know your college's president.

The president is the institutional leader who sets the vision for the college and, depending on the size of the college and the way it is governed, he or she may have a profound influence on the institution's tone as well. In my former capacity with UNCF, I visited over 30 historically black colleges and universities (HBCUs), oftentimes meeting with the president and senior academic officer such as the provost. I also became very close to the President of MIT, Susan Hockfield, while I served as Associate Dean of Undergraduate Education there. Here's what I discovered: To a man or woman, the one experience that presidents miss is the regular contact with students. Their days are packed with meetings, fundraising trips, and phone calls, and as a result they get minimal student contact, unless it's formally scheduled. So they relish opportunities to slow down and be reminded about why they've chosen to occupy that office in the first place: to educate the next generation of scholars, lawyers, engineers, doctors, teachers, etc.

Knowing this, I encourage my advisees to visit with the college president. Set up a brief appointment and tell him or her that you want to introduce yourself and hear about their vision for the college. And before your meeting? Again, do your research. Study the president's background. Where is he from? Where did she earn her undergraduate degrees? His graduate degrees? What was her research specialty? If you can get a copy of the president's inauguration speech, or view it online, do it. Come prepared with a handful of questions, but be poised to listen. Asking "How would you recommend I get the most out of my time here?" is an easy, all-purpose question. Some presidents are so eager to engage in this way that you might find they'll talk for the whole allotted time. That's OK. If you didn't get to all of your questions, mention that and set up another appointment, perhaps in a month's time.

Getting to know your president is one key to making the vertical Connections Shift. As I hinted a moment ago, the financial-aid office is another.

## "Show Me the Money": Get to Know Your Financial Aid Office

In the movie *Jerry McGuire*, Rod Tidwell, the star football player played by Cuba Gooding, Jr., made famous the line, "Show me the money!" Money plays a significant role in your ability to stay in school. A UNCF analysis determined that a student attending one of its 37 member institutions is more likely to leave college in the latter years — junior and senior year — because of an inability to pay the tuition and fees than for any other reason.

As a result, you definitely want to make a good connection with the staff in the financial-aid office. They should know you on a first-name basis, not because they see you begging, or as hostile towards them, but because you and they should be dealing with your financial situation as a team. If you apply for financial aid during or soon after completing the admission process, your first experience with this office is the aid package you'll receive — grants, loans, scholarships you can apply for — to help close the gap between what the college costs and your family's ability to pay that amount from your own means and through other scholarships you may already have earned.

Once you arrive on campus, set up an appointment to introduce yourself to the financial-aid officers so you can understand the details of your aid package. How much of it is work-study, which requires you to work during the semester? What percentage of the package consists of loans? When will you be expected to pay them back? At what interest rates? How will you get notified when a payment is due, or a refund check comes in? These are the types of questions you should come prepared to ask.

But more importantly, you are forging a relationship, putting a face to a name. You want them to know a little about you, that you are more than an entry on a computer screen. You'll learn more about them, too. Some financial-aid offices, for instance, have a full-time scholarship coordinator in place. The office receives many scholarship announcements over the course of the year. As you get to know the staff, you may come to mind when new scholarships are available. It can't hurt for them to know you.

## "Help" is Not a Four-Letter Word: Use the College's Support Services

### Tutoring Centers

Most colleges offer tutoring and writing help for students to bring them up to speed with their content knowledge, and with their overall academic skills. Take advantage of that help. Dr. Freeman Hrabowski, the president of the University of Maryland Baltimore County, tells his highly selective Meyerhoff Scholars that if they don't have an A in a particular course — even if they have a strong B or an A- — they need tutoring. (I've added this for my advisees: "And if you *do* have an A, you should *be* tutoring.") "Help" is not a four-letter word! You should embrace the idea of getting help, a theme I hope I drilled home in last chapter's discussion about the "growth mindset." Are you open to improving? You ought to be. You need to be.

Regardless of how you're doing at the moment, you should make a connection with the tutoring center, whether it is located in the department of your major, or in another department, or even as part of a central student-affairs office. Once again, get to know them early — *before* you need them — so that if and when times get tough, you already have a relationship with the staff. And who knows? Down the road, you may have an opportunity to be on the other side of the desk, and actually get paid to tutor. Getting paid to share your knowledge, to develop teaching skills, and to gain true mastery of your subject matter? It's — pardon the pun — a no-brainer.

*The Writing Center*

I'd make a similar connection recommendation about the college's writing center. Recall the study I mentioned earlier about students who were given a choice to view the papers of those who did better, or did worse, than they did. The fixed-mindset students only wanted to see the papers of the peers who did worse so as to preserve their own feeling of superiority, even if they did poorly themselves. The growth-mindset students, by contrast, accepted the challenge of seeing papers that received higher grades than theirs.

They wanted to get better.

That's the mindset you need when you visit the writing center. Writing is the sticking point for a lot of students because many high schools simply don't prepare them for college-level writing. More commonly, your high-school English class was overcrowded, or the teacher's workload was such that they were reluctant to assign long papers because of the extra burden of grading them. And so (as happened to me, you'll recall, during my summer "bridge" program), submitting that first college paper might have been a shock, both in how much writing you were expected to do, and in how low a grade you received.

Like those fixed-mindset students, your tendency might be to shrink back and hide your writing grade if you did more poorly than you expected or hoped. You might simply vow to yourself that you'll do better next time. In fact, if you're honest with yourself, you don't know what "doing better next time" requires. That's where the writing center (and, for that matter, the tutoring center) comes in. Get to know the folks whose job it is to give you an objective opinion about your writing ability, and specific tips on how you can get better.

Give it one semester. Forget your pride or your concerns about what your friends will think. Walk in to introduce yourself and set up an appointment. Schedule the visit at least a few days before the first draft of that next assignment is due and learn what resources the center has available. These folks are experts at what they do. You're not. (At least when it comes to writing.) You can always learn something from them, but more importantly, getting to know them and working with them will build your confidence. Trust me on this.

### The Career Services Office

Another important resource on campus is the career-services office. This is the place that typically helps you find and pursue job opportunities, either through summer or academic-year internships while you're still in school, or through permanent employment once you've graduated. As was true with the tutoring and writing centers, I suggest you go in and set up an appointment with a career counselor to familiarize yourself with the office's range of services, and also to help them get to know you.

These offices are flooded with internship and other summer opportunities by companies and alumni. The more this office knows you and your interests, the more likely you'll get a shot at these opportunities. (I remember a notice I received my freshman year about a summer internship that paid me more than my parents were making combined. That was possible only because I was already a known entity to the folks in career services.) And looking even further ahead? You may not know what you want to do for full-time work when you graduate. The career office can help you sort out your options.

So how do you make your first visit to career services as productive as possible?

Arrive prepared, with a set of questions:

- "What kind of jobs do graduates from this college typically find?"
- "What types of careers are typical for graduates in my major?"
- "How can I best position myself for a summer internship?"

- "What grade point average and set of experiences do students [in the case of internships] or graduates typically have to be competitive in this field?"

The career-services office may also be very useful in helping you decide on a major. I used to administer the Strong Interest Inventory to my freshmen advisees; it's one of the most widely used career-planning tools that helps students and professionals discover their preferred major or career based on their interests and preferences. Most colleges' career-services offices can offer you this assessment, or one like it, to help inform your choice of major. Take advantage of the opportunity.

Making the connections with career services early in your college career will help you apply what Steven Covey, the author of *Seven Habits of Highly Effective* People, suggests: "Begin with the end in mind." In other words, in whatever tasks you pursue, be thinking about what you want to accomplish or the outcome you desire; you'll become more focused and motivated if you start with a clear vision of the finish line. By visiting career services, you can gain a clearer perspective about what you'd like to do once you are through with school. This, in turn, will make you more purposeful as a student, particularly in influencing your course selection each semester. That "long view" may even provide you the extra motivation to push through difficult academic periods. And speaking of the long view...

## SEE YOURSELF GRADUATING

In addition to frequenting the career-services office while I was in college, I used to watch graduations and imagine hearing my name called and walking across the stage. In fact, some years later that same practice — seeing graduates in their caps and gowns lining up near my office every June — inspired me to go back to school to get a doctorate in education. The day that I walked across the stage, while an exhilarating experience, was also strangely familiar because I had done it so many times in my mind.

Bottom line is this: Find your motivation.

## FIND A MENTOR. (FIND MORE THAN ONE.)

In Chapter I, I introduced three of my college mentors: Dr. Clarence Williams, my freshman advisor; Dr. Bill MacLaurin, the Director of the Office of Minority Education; and Nels Armstrong, the Associate Director of Admissions. And while they happened to all be African American males, which naturally drew me to them, they brought different styles to their role as mentors and played key roles at various points in my undergraduate and professional career. They also had something else in common: They all had my best interest in mind. The takeaway here: One mentor is good, more can be even better. Build a *network* of mentors.

Studies have shown that mentoring is effective for helping students overcome the barriers that prevent them from being successful in college. Mentoring also reduces the chances of students leaving school after the first year, and increases self-confidence. One of the most effective mentoring relationships described in the research "entails friendship, guidance, counseling, a warm and genuine smile at times, referrals, and encouragement; it also means playing student advocate, navigator, proofreader, and alarm clock as needed".[11]

That's how I would describe my own mentors' contributions in college. (Except for the alarm-clock function. None of them woke me up in the mornings, but they all awakened me to many promising possibilities.) Among your faculty and administrators, you're looking for one or more kind and caring adults with whom you can connect on multiple levels — academically, professionally, spiritually, and/or personally. These mentors will certainly help you handle the vertical part of the Connections Shift.

Now, what about the horizontal part? What about peer connections? I'll tackle that next.

## MAKING THE PEER CONNECTIONS

I met Gerry Baron on the Greyhound bus to Boston heading up to campus for freshman orientation. I got on at the first stop, in Hempstead,

Long Island. He got on the bus at the second stop, in Queens. Four hours later, by the time we arrived in Boston, we were fast friends. I had briefed him about all of the people I met during the previous summer while attending the summer bridge program, and I learned a lot about his family. That serendipitous meeting led to a long-term friendship. Though we live in separate cities, we still stay in touch now more than 30 years later!

Gerry and I were connected at the hip for the first two years of college before our academic paths diverged, Gerry's toward mechanical engineering, and mine toward materials science and engineering. Still, we lived in the same dorm, went to the same parties, and even liked the same girls (though Gerry mostly won that competition). Later that year, we also became close to two other freshmen, Gordon Wright and Patrick Gerdes, both of whom also lived in Chocolate City.

Even though we were close, we would "snap" on each other all of the time. The jokes never got too personal, but they were always given to exaggeration. The other thing the joking did, in a strange way, was to solidify our knowledge of what we were learning. All of us were taking freshman physics (mechanics), the bane of most freshmen at MIT. It was the hardest course because you had to learn to use calculus to derive the very equations you needed to solve the problems, rather than simply plugging in values to preexisting formulas. I remember during the unit on relativity that our joking got really funny, but it also solidified our understanding of Einstein's breakthrough theory. You see, it turns out, as an object travels near the speed of light — 186,282 miles per second — it will move more slowly, and shorten in length, from the point of view of an observer on Earth. So, in a hypothetical situation, an astronaut who left the Earth in a spacecraft that travels near the speed of light, upon his or her return to Earth, would have aged differently than those who stayed on terra firma. Heady stuff!

I remember one lunch right after class; we were all trying to get our heads around these concepts, when one of the guys started to talk about the other's girlfriend. "Man, if you took her out on a spaceship at the speed of light and brought her back, she wouldn't look any better than when she left." That "snap" was followed by another proclamation even more bizarre. (Did I mention we were kidding? Those of us who had girlfriends were very satisfied with their looks, but this was the way 18-year-olds talked.) Looking back on it, though, the offensive nature of our comments aside, the joking was solidifying our knowledge of the concepts, while providing some fun along the way.

You need friends with whom you can joke, but who are not ashamed to talk about their schoolwork as well. With some minority populations, and certainly this was my experience in high school until I found my posse, talking about schoolwork is off-limits within the social circle. That's wrong. If that's the way your posse rolls, then you should find or form your own posse.

## "THE PACT"

The best example I know of this was exemplified by three doctors who, when they were in high school, formed a pact.

Three young men who grew up in the streets of Newark, NJ, decided to commit to helping each other become doctors. After bouts with crime, surviving drug-addicted parents, a gang-infested neighborhood, and even jail, Sampson Davis, George Jenkins, and Rameck Hunt supported each other through college, medical and dental school. They do so even now as they travel throughout the country inspiring young people to dream big regardless of their circumstances. They helped each other get through their education and training; none of them was allowed to drop out or perform poorly on tests. (Without knowing it, that's much the same kind of pact my "bus friend" Gerry and I had established during our first two years of college: a commitment to see each other through.)

For these three sons of Newark, their healthy competition helped each of them become better students, never miss a class or an assignment, and pass their board exams. Their compelling story is captured in the book titled (naturally!) *The Pact: Three Young Men Make a Promise and Fulfill a Dream.*

Drs. Davis, Jenkins and Hunt had formed a posse that kept them motivated and also gave them a buffer against forces potentially destructive to their dream. What forces do I mean? Well, just look to physics. Newton's Third Law of Motion says that every action, or force, is opposed by an equal and opposite reaction or force. I've found that this same notion can apply to the drive for success: When you decide to set aspirations high and pursue a life course that challenges prevailing norms, you will be opposed, either internally by your own doubts, fears or discomfort, or by other people. By forming a pact, these three young men built an inviolable buffer against those destructive forces.

When I discovered the book, and their story, some years later, I knew I would use it for my seminar. After reading the book a second time, I pulled out specific attributes that made their pact so successful:

- They had a common goal — to become doctors;
- They had a lot in common even beyond their academic and professional pursuits;
- They operated out of a shared value system — they would function as a group, never miss a class or an assignment, and never leave one another behind;
- They used positive peer pressure to spur them on to perform well;
- There was a healthy competition between them to outperform one another;
- They were not concerned about embarrassing each other when they needed to buckle down, nor were they embarrassed to ask for help;
- They studied and played together, breaking down the academic and social barriers;
- They taught each other;
- They held each other accountable for their grades;

KARL W. REID, ED.D.

They allowed each individual to be himself, bringing each young man's unique personality and style into the relationship. As a college administrator and freshman seminar leader, I had my incoming freshmen read the first two chapters of *The Pact* before we even met. And their first seminar assignment — a group assignment — was to formulate an "Achievement Contract," the pact that would encapsulate the shared goals that would inspire and guide *them* over the next four years of college. When they were done, I typed up the terms and had each young man sign the agreement. Then I made copies, which each of them placed at the front of the seminar binder so that each week they'd be reminded of their commitments to each other.

It worked. There were times over the five years that I had to remind them of their contract, though that was rare. To their credit, since these were their own terms, they internalized and owned them. Here's an example of an Achievement Contract for one of my advising groups:

1. Maintain a cumulative grade point average (GPA) of 4.5 (out of 5.0) or better.
2. Graduate with a bachelor's degree in four (4) years or less.
3. Attend all classes, recitations, seminars, and appointments *on time*, unless physically unable.
4. Do all readings before class meetings and complete/submit no late work.
5. Pursue graduate studies (Master's or Doctoral) within one (1) year of graduation with the bachelor's degree.
6. Commit to and perform at least one (1) sustainable community-service project/activity per academic year.
7. Establish a relationship with at least four (4) people who could potentially serve as recommenders (at least one of whom being a professor) per academic year.

That was one group's shared goals, one group's commitments to one another. What would you add, or delete, if you were coming up with an agreement for you and your friends? It's worth thinking about.

And here's one more question: Who would those friends be?

### DISCOVER AND EXPAND YOUR POSSE

Just like the three aspiring doctors, you need to find folks for your posse who are mutually supportive in reaching your individual and collective goals. It won't all happen at once. Friendships and social bonds evolve and spread over time, like concentric circles expanding.

Unless you know someone from your high school, your first physical connection in college is typically with a roommate. Facebook and other social media will enable you to meet hundreds of students in your class (and upperclassmen and alumni, too) even before you arrive on campus, but your roommate will tend to be your first strong connection. Then, as you immerse yourself in the campus community, particularly if you are on an athletic team or join a club such as a Bible study group, a debate team, or another student group, your social network will start to grow.

Over time, your connections will include those with whom you share classes, especially when you form study groups. Then, once you declare a major, you'll likely be spending more time with your "major mates" than anyone else, unless you're playing an intercollegiate sport. Finally, though this may happen earlier, a boyfriend or girlfriend will bring you into entirely new circles.

I say all of that to suggest that your peer connections will, and should continue to, evolve throughout your college years. While all of them won't, and needn't, serve an academic or career-building purpose, you should be careful in making the peer portion of the Connections Shift not to allow any connection to pull you off your path toward academic, personal, and career success. In many social networks, we make friends because of the social currency it brings us. However, when those connections draw you away from being proud of your academic pursuits, then *you need to change your network*. If your peers make you uncomfortable celebrating an "A" on an exam, then you're running with the wrong posse. Period!

## GET OUTSIDE YOUR COMFORT ZONE: EXPAND BEYOND YOUR RACIAL, GENDER, OR RELIGIOUS GROUP

I made a huge mistake when I got to college. I joined just about every organization that had the word "black" in it — The Black Student Union, the National Society of Black Engineers, the Black Christian Fellowship. If it didn't have the word "black" in it, it had "chocolate" (like my living group, Chocolate City) or had an African name, like the Kuumba Singers. I even attended an African Methodist Episcopal Church simply because it had the word "African" in it. I was at a place in my own racial and ethnic development where I needed to retreat into a place of "identity safety," as researcher Claude Steele labels it, a place that was socially familiar to me, and where I didn't feel like I had to explain myself. I knew the rules — those social norms that govern how we interact — because I'd grown up in the world dictated by African American rules and values. There's nothing wrong, as Dr. Steele states, with choosing to retreat into a comfortable place.

But joining all of these groups wasn't my mistake. My mistake was joining *only* these groups. As I said, being a part of these groups — the people I met, the bonds that I formed, and the leadership skills I developed — was critical to my social, personal and professional growth and development. But until my senior year, I failed to branch out to other communities or groups that did *not* have "black" in the title.

It was participating in the Efficacy Institute in my senior year that called my social myopia into question. It caused me to ask why I had limited myself to just the African American groups and social circles. From that point forward, I reached out to acquaintances from my classes and labs that I had encountered but never cultivated over my earlier years at school. (I even reached out to other black students who, for whatever reason, felt alienated from the larger black community.) Sometimes we sat down together for lunch. Other times it was for coffee. In the ensuing months, as I undertook this new outreach, I learned so much about these other students and about my university. For one thing, I learned what I was missing: There was a whole world there on campus — a world of fraternities and sororities, of clubs and committees — I had failed to take advantage of. There were opportunities for research, and even majors, that I could have pursued that were closer to my emerging interests.

Don't get me wrong. I had a rich experience as it was, even if it was somewhat one-dimensional. But, like moving from an old TV for the first time, I really didn't know what I'd been missing until I saw high definition. My college experience was a low-def experience because I had limited myself to a narrowly defined set of organizations and friends.

## EXPAND YOUR SOCIAL CIRCLE EACH YEAR

Research shows that students who have an expanded social circle are typically those with a mature sense of their racial and ethnic identity. Making connections across differences eliminates unconscious biases and leads to better and more meaningful understanding about people. We all have biases. However, the more meaningful interactions we have with those who are different from us, the more likely these biases will be challenged and eliminated. I remember how my views about the LBGTQ community changed after I spent time with a friend who "came out" well into our friendship.

Greater intellectual growth has been tied to greater diversity, because as your thoughts and beliefs are challenged by a wider and more varied set of friends and colleagues, you are more likely to gain a broader point of view, making your opinions much more nuanced. In short, diversity can stimulate the "growth mindset" we discussed earlier.

Whatever your situation — whether you were like me, needing to retreat into identity safety by race or ethnicity, by gender or geography, by hobby or major — recognize that you should do so just for a season.

"Retreat" should never be a permanent state. In fact, I encourage you each year, or even each semester, to expand your social circle a bit. Join a group you had not been a part of previously. Sign up for a campus committee, or run for office. All of these will help expand your peer connections and foster development of your social skills, because you'll be forced to interact with those outside of your predefined group. Trust me on this. You will learn more and you will gain new perspectives, all of which you will be able to use to enrich your posse. Who knows? Your posse may grow, and *all* of you will benefit.

## Consider Joining a Study Group

I was not a big fan of study groups in college. Early on, when I had trouble finding my bearings, I sat in a few study groups for physics. I found myself writing answers that others had solved because I had no clue about the material. I struggled to understand the questions, let alone where to go in my notes and textbooks to find answers. I felt like I was learning a foreign language. My goal at that point was simply to finish the problem sets, and not necessarily to learn the material. My "fixed mindset" kicked in. Consequently, despite getting reasonable grades on my homework, I got killed on my exams.

Later, when I found my bearings and began to apply the deep-dive learning method, I thought study groups would be a waste of time. My friends would get together for hours to finish a problem set or prepare for exams, but so many superfluous topics came up during the discussion — from the latest party, to who's dating whom — that they would spend more than twice the time I used to finish the work. With these two extremes as my models, it's not surprising that I rarely participated in study groups while I was an undergraduate.

Years later, I read the transcript of a speech given by University of Texas professor Uri Treisman about a study he conducted while a graduate student at the University of California, Berkeley, in the 1970s. As a TA for a calculus course, he discovered that no more than two African American students over the previous decade had received a B- or better in first-term calculus. He then conducted a study to determine why so many racial minorities were failing the course and ultimately dropping out of mathematics, and in some cases, out of the university. He wanted to test certain hypotheses, conventional explanations among faculty and administration for why these students were failing: lack of motivation; inadequate academic preparation; inadequate family support for academic pursuits; difficulty for those from low-income families and neighborhoods to adjust to college (all of which were later proven wrong).

With their permission, he and his colleagues conducted an 18-month study of about 40 students (20 African American and 20 Chinese American), including an observational study in which he videotaped African American and Chinese students as they studied and participated in other social activities. He chose the Chinese students as a control group because they were consistently above-average performers in the freshman course.

When Professor Treisman studied the videotape, he noticed that while members of both groups spent a fair amount of time studying alone (6-8 hours weekly for African American students, 8-10 hours for Chinese), the Chinese students spent an additional 4-6 hours per week together in social settings over meals talking about their academics. They checked each other's work, discussed assignments, and worked problems from old exams in preparation for upcoming tests. They were also joined by older Chinese-American students who guided their discussion. For them, there was no dividing line between the social realm and the academic realm. It blended together, as the figure below illustrates.

## TREISMAN'S FINDINGS: ASIAN STUDENTS

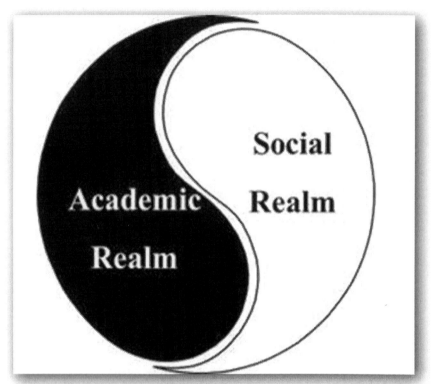

STATE OF BALANCE In all aspects of life a state of
balance should exist between the opposing forces of Ying
(Academic Realm) and Yang (Social Realm)

One result of this blending of social and academic conversation: The Chinese students always knew where they stood in class, and relative to other students in the class.

The African American students, on the other hand, while they also gathered for social reasons, rarely discussed academics during those gatherings. In this community, there seemed to be a clear demarcation between their academic and social worlds, and never the two should meet, as illustrated below.

## TREISMAN'S FINDINGS: AFRICAN AMERICAN STUDENTS

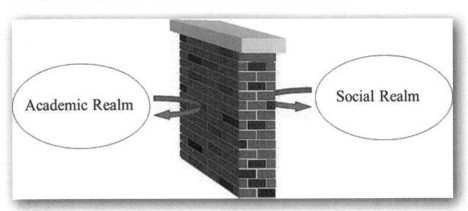

There was no evidence that they even joked about their academic subjects, as my friends and I did over meals when we were learning Relativity. As a result, they didn't know where they stood in class and relative to other students, and consequently were often shocked when they received their grades.

Dr. Treisman went on to create the Mathematics Workshop Program, where he would assemble groups of 20 to 25 students to develop deeper understanding of the concepts taught in the math class itself. The problems they solved were more difficult than those that were covered in the recitations. The sessions would be facilitated by a graduate student who would not lecture but rather would lead problem-solving sessions designed not only to help students understand concepts in the current course, but to build a foundation for future math and science courses. Most importantly, there was an air of high expectations in this community-based setting. Here, the academic and social integration was employed in smaller, more intense, but very supportive study groups.

The results were stunning. In the first year, over 50 percent of African American participants earned a grade of B- or better in first-year calculus, compared to just 21 percent of black students who did not participate in the workshop. Most importantly, four times more African American students graduated with math-based majors than those African Americans who did not participate.[12]

## How I Changed My Mind About the Power of Study Groups

When I went to graduate school, I struggled in one class that required a lot of reading. It was the History of Higher Education and we had to read a book a week, books that ranged in length from 200 to 400 pages. Because I worked full time, and still am a relatively slow (I like to use the term "methodical") reader, it took me all week to get through each of these books. I was always prepared for class, but I had little time for my other classes, my health, and my family.

About five weeks into the course, several students invited me to join them to discuss potential topics for our upcoming paper. About a half a dozen of us went around the table pitching our ideas for the paper, giving and getting constructive feedback about the topics, the themes, and the sources we planned to use. This was enormously helpful because it helped to refine my approach and my thought process.

After the discussion, they suddenly switched gears and started to talk about the week's readings. I asked what they were doing. They explained that because they all had so much work to do, they collectively decided that they would have to work together to share the readings. Each student would read a chapter or two in detail, write up a detailed summary, then the group would come together two days before class to present their reading — chapter by chapter. The meetings would take about 90 minutes to go through the whole book. Everyone would walk away with a written summary of each chapter and the benefit of an oral discussion.

I had an epiphany, an "Aha!" moment. This experience, coupled with what I had read about Uri Treisman's work, changed my view of study groups. Used well, I decided, they could be helpful.

I then tried my emerging theory on a subsequent class in microeconomics. I organized a study group that was scheduled to meet for

90 minutes two days before the problem sets were due. One of the other group members reserved a conference room on campus. I urged everyone to become familiar with the problems and begin to work out solutions on their own. Prior to coming together, they were to answer the following questions:

- What will be your approach to solving this problem?
- How do you know this approach is correct?
- What portion of the lecture or the reading did you reference?

The group was not to come to the meeting with answers to the problems, but to be prepared to discuss *their approach*. We all sought consensus on how to solve each problem, but we didn't finish the problem set during our meeting. Instead, we would all later finish the problem sets on our own.

If there were persistent questions that could not be solved or for which we could not come to consensus, we had enough time (because, remember, we would meet at least two days before the due date) for a volunteer to go to the professor or the TA to get answers and then email them back to the group.

It ran like clockwork. Not only did we all do well in the course, but most importantly, we learned the material deeply. Working on our own, followed by the 90 minutes together, and then finishing up on our own was the winning formula for properly utilizing study groups and, most importantly, getting to mastery.

So: What had I learned from the experience? What makes a study group effective?

For starters, you have to realize that the study group itself is just one step in a three-step process aimed at mastering the subject. The three steps go like this:

**Individual work → Group work (study group)→ Individual work**

And it's vital to give attention to the steps that precede and follow the study group.

Here's what I mean: For a study group to be effective, everyone in the group must also be prepared to do work on his or her own before and after the group meets. The working group should not be where you get most of your work done; you'll never master the material that way. As I mentioned earlier, giving yourself focus, reviewing the material on your own, and beginning to work the problems are all essential steps toward deepening your recall, increasing your ability to synthesize the material, and preparing for the study-group discussion. Only by completing these steps are you are prepared, when you finally get together, to contribute to your colleagues' learning, crystallize your own learning, or correct your understanding of the material.

So those are the steps at the front end. And at the back end? Well, it's once again time for individual effort.

And here's what I mean by *that*: It's important that you finish the assignment on your own, not with the group. This ensures that you crystallize your understanding; you're able to take theory and concepts and apply them to the problem at hand. If you don't lock that in, you run the risk of having the experiences I had early on: good homework grades but poor exam scores because I hadn't synthesized the material in my own mind.

This approach — individual work at the final stage — also minimizes the chances that you can be accused of plagiarism. Finishing assignments together increases the likelihood of you and your classmates coming up with solutions that look identical, putting you all on the professor's watch list or, more damagingly, leading to a sanction of some kind.

In short, view the study group as a valuable *middle step* toward mastery. Think of the entire process as a sandwich. Working individually before and after the study group meets is the bread, and the study group is the meat (or peanut butter and jelly, for those of you who are vegetarians). Now, let's turn to this question: What makes for a good sandwich?

### Don't think of study groups as "remedial"

One essential element of a successful study group is the attitude you and your colleagues adopt toward it before you even get started. Effective study groups should *not* be oriented toward remediation. In other words, they should not have the reputation or practice for bringing students "up to speed" or overcoming deficits. Rather, like the Treisman workshops, they should be considered opportunities for students who want to excel! This is one reason I advocate creating study groups at the *beginning* of the semester rather than waiting to pull students in after they're in trouble. Everyone who joins them must want to do well in that course, not just receive a passing grade. Having, and communicating, this attitude will attract all kinds of students and avoid giving your group the reputation that it can benefit only students who "need help." Such a label will cause both those who need study groups most, and those who are doing well, to avoid them, and thus defeat the fundamental purpose of the group: the pursuit of mastery for *all* students.

That's the positive attitude you need. What about the logistics?

### Set a day and time

Groups should set a specific day and time to meet each week. I suggest you meet two or three days before weekly assignments are due, so there's sufficient lead time for each individual to begin work on the problem set or assignment before the group meets. (Everyone should have begun that work, of course; as I will recommend later, you should begin assignments on the day they're given.)

Meeting at least two days before the assignment is due, to repeat, will give the group enough time to put questions from the meeting to your TA or professor with sufficient time to receive and make use of the answers. Finally, a specific time "window" reduces the chance that the team will waste time. Knowing that you only have 90 minutes or two hours will lessen the likelihood that you get into longwinded or irrelevant conversations about superfluous topics.

*Admit no more than 4 or 5 members*
Unlike the Treisman workshops, which had 20 to 25 students apiece and were facilitated by a graduate student, I don't think your study group should have more than a half-dozen members. Four to five would be optimum to ensure that everyone is engaged and held accountable for doing their share of the work. Larger groups allow participants to hide what they don't know or didn't do. Smaller groups, by contrast, oblige everyone to participate and make sense of the material for themselves. Once again, the goal is not just accountability, but mastery of the material.

*Hold everyone accountable*
But accountability is certainly part of the mix. Accountability is an essential component to make study groups work most effectively. Each group member should come prepared to discuss his or her approach to the problems. No one should be allowed to chronically slack off, or repeatedly miss the group. Invariably, one or another member will have one of those occasional crunch weeks and arrive for the meeting unprepared. The group should willingly carry them for that week. But these instances should be the exception, not the rule. And when group members are unprepared, they should still participate. Not only will they learn from the others, but they may still be able to contribute from the information they've gleaned from the lecture, the notes, or the readings.

Members who repeatedly slack off should be asked to leave the group or recommit to its goals and standards. There should be no exceptions. Everyone must see themselves as a part of a whole, a contributor rather than just a bystander, or even worse, an exploiter of others' work.

*Be honest and open*

What's needed in these and other situations is openness and honesty. You may have had a long paper to write for another class, or you may have been on an extended road trip with your athletic team. As a result, you haven't done the necessary work for your next study group. These things happen. It's important, though, that the group knows up front that you'll arrive unprepared. Don't "fake it to make it." People will know. It's much better to square with them. "Folks, I didn't get a chance to go over the problems this week. I'll participate as much as I can, but I'll be ready next week." Your group might even want to automatically assign you, the unprepared person, to lead the following week's discussion. It's another way to hold people to their promises.

I recall times in my microeconomics study group that I showed up unprepared. I felt like I was watching a tennis match as the intellectual ball got batted around. I did learn something, and finished my problem set that week, though it was much more difficult because I didn't have the benefit of participating fully in the discussion. Still, not being prepared felt uncomfortable, and I didn't want to feel that feeling again. Neither should you.

*Rotate the leaders*

And finally, speaking of assigning someone to lead the next week's discussion: I recommend that leaders rotate each week so there is shared responsibility for the group's smooth functioning, and that one person isn't always seen as the bad guy. Sharing responsibility will build empathy for that week's leader, increase the likelihood that others will keep the group discussion on track, and cut down on troublemakers.

Each week's leader will have the responsibility to keep the group moving. Occasionally, the group will find itself distracted, particularly if something happens on campus, in the news, or in sports that everyone is talking about. That's fine. But it should be the leader's responsibility to rein everyone in when necessary, and to make sure the group is getting through the work.

We've now discussed the Attitude and Connection Shifts that are necessary for you to work smarter in college. It's almost time to turn to the final, vital, piece of the puzzle: the Behavior Shift. Before we do, though, let's summarize the key points of this chapter.

## WORKING SMARTER TAKEAWAYS: THE CONNECTIONS SHIFT

### MAKE CONNECTIONS WITH FACULTY

- Building strong relationships with faculty members increases the likelihood of confidence-building interactions;
- Visit your professor early in the semester, before any work is graded;
- Bring a friend to meet with the professor if you need moral support;
- Before meeting with your professor, study his or her bio to see if you can make a personal connection, and arrive at your meeting with your questions in mind;
- Visit your professor or TA at least once a week;
- Make use of the professor's office hours, or (sparingly) the professor's "board time" before or after class, to ask quick, clarifying questions;
- Never miss an exam review;
- Seek opportunities to do research with faculty members.

### MAKE CONNECTIONS WITH ADMINISTRATORS

- Reach out to key administrators: Introduce yourself to the president and other senior officials, including the head of the department of your declared or likely major;

- Familiarize yourself with the financial-aid and career-services offices;
- Don't dismiss administrative assistants in your department headquarters and other offices — get to know them;
- Get to know the tutoring and writing centers on campus; remember, your goal is constant improvement;
- Find one or more mentors, kind and caring adults with whom you can connect on various levels.

## MAKE CONNECTIONS WITH PEERS

- Find the right kinds of friends and form a pact to keep you motivated, accountable, and focused on your goals;
- Form, then keep expanding, your posse beyond your own racial, ethnic, and gender background.

## MAKE YOUR STUDY GROUP EFFECTIVE

- Use your study group to pitch and debate topics for future papers, and to review early drafts of your work;
- Recognize that study groups are one step in a three-step learning process to maximize learning: Study alone, then in a group, then alone;
- Set a specific day and time to meet, at least two days prior to the assignment due date;
- Invite no more than 4 to 5 members to be part of your study group;
- Hold everyone accountable to do their share of the work;
- Be honest and open about your ability to hold up your end of the bargain;
- Rotate the study group's leadership.

What's your attitude? Who — and how varied — are your connections? And now...

What actions should you take, what habits should you adopt, to be successful in college (and in the workplace)? That's our third "shift."

# CHAPTER 4

## THE BEHAVIOR SHIFT

## INTRODUCTION

WOULD IT SURPRISE you to learn that, in a recent national survey, only 50 percent of all students polled said they had developed effective study habits in college?[13] This chapter is designed to fill in the gaps — for the 50 percent who say they've never developed effective approaches to studying, for those who *say* they have but really haven't, and for those about to begin college who want to get off to a good start.

The deep-dive learning approach — what I call the Behavior Shift — was born out of my own experience in college, and that of scores of high school and college students with whom I've worked for over 20 years. I've also included elements of some of the best study approaches that I've encountered, as well as the latest brain research on how best to learn.

## WORKING SMARTER: THE BEHAVIOR SHIFT

The Behavior Shift to Working Smarter begins with this premise: It's better to study alone than to study in groups. At least that's what the research says. In fact, the more students study alone, the more intellectual, problem-solving, critical thinking and writing skills they develop.[14] But wait! In our previous chapter, didn't I make the case for the importance of study groups? It seems contradictory to advocate for both working alone and in groups. It seems like I'm "writing" out of both sides of my mouth.

So which is it? Here's my answer: *It depends on what you're doing.* Study groups are critical for answering questions and developing mastery — in other words, for reinforcing material you've already begun to absorb alone. You can't solve deep, complex problems without first acquiring a deep factual and procedural knowledge of the material. (Call it "First Learning.") And for that purpose, working alone is the way to go. Study groups are an inefficient and ineffective vehicle for learning new material. Period.

## SET S.M.A.R.T. GOALS

There's a second premise in this chapter, too: It's absolutely vital for you to set goals. Goals compel you to focus your effort. Goals are a prerequisite of motivation and ultimately for developing the "deep dive" approach to learning I will show you. In Chapter 2, I discussed how some students develop low expectations about their performance in a particular class ("I probably won't do better than a 'C'.") The researchers called that *defensive pessimism*. Other students — the *strategic optimists* — set high goals for class and are disappointed if they don't earn a grade no worse than slightly below a very high bar.

Let me ask you: On any given day in that class, if you got to observe the two groups studying — the defensive pessimists and the strategic optimists — which group would be more focused and put in more effort? The strategic optimists, of course. That's the power of goal setting. High, challenging goals keep you focused on the task and lead to better results.

So how do you set a goal, and what type of goals should you set? I like the acronym "S.M.A.R.T." that I've borrowed from countless thought leaders, including Paul Meyer in his book, "Attitude is Everything."[15] He suggests setting goals that are effective and measurable. It's not much help to set a goal that says, "I want to become a better student." How do you measure "better"? Study better? Get better grades? Make better use of your time? No, your goals should be S.M.A.R.T.:

- **S**pecific: That is, they should not be general goals as in the example I gave, but should clearly state what you want to accomplish. For instance, "I will finish the year with a grade point average above 3.4 for the semester."
- **M**easurable: There must be concrete criteria against which you can evaluate whether or not you've achieved the goal. A 3.4 GPA is a measurable goal. "Becoming a better person" is not.
- **A**ttainable: A goal to safely and successfully ski down the hardest trail the first time you strap on skis is not "attainable" (unless you ride down on someone's back). Likewise, your goals should be realistic and reachable, but also at least somewhat challenging. They must stretch your abilities and not be too easy and, therefore, meaningless.
- **R**elevant: As a student, your goals should pertain to your academic and career-oriented experiences. Setting a GPA goal or boosting your typing speed by a measurable amount are relevant goals toward achieving success in college.
- **T**ime-bound: Make sure your goals have a timeline, deadline or a target date for completion. Doing so will ensure a focus. Have you ever noticed how the intensity peaks at the end of a game when time is about to run out? That's what time-bound goals do; they raise the level of intensity, and prompt you to double down on your efforts as the deadline approaches.

## SHARE YOUR GOALS

I've added another letter to S.M.A.R.T. Goals, and that's a second "S." Effective goals have S.M.A.R.T.S. That final "S" is for "Sharing." Effective goals are shared with others who can hold you accountable for achieving them. What good is it if you set goals, then keep them to yourself? It'll be too easy to abandon them if no one but you knows about them. But if you share them with someone, or even multiple "someones", you trust — "I'm going to get a 3.4 GPA this semester"— then they can call you on them. (If they don't, then reread the Connections Shift chapter and find another posse!)

I had my freshmen advisees set goals for their first semester, for their entire freshman year, and for their four years in college. They'd share their goals among their peers and we would apply the S.M.A.R.T. test to each of the goals. By the time the third guy had shared his goals, the group had internalized this approach and the participants would challenge each other on whether or not the goals were specific, measurable, attainable, relevant, and time-bound. They knew a S.M.A.R.T. goal when they saw one!

## REVISIT AND REVISE YOUR GOALS

What good is it to establish goals and never review how you are doing, or how you did, to achieve them? Doing that is like training for a marathon but never recording your training time — how can you be sure you're making progress?

At the beginning of the second semester, I had my freshman advisees revisit their first-semester goals in front of the other guys in the seminar. I asked them to recite their goals, share with the group how they did against their goals, and what strategies they'd employ to improve their performance in the coming semester. Here, the Connections Shift matters. The students formed an accountability group that wasn't shy about reminding the members of their original goals. ("Didn't you say you weren't going to miss a class? What happened?")

It's possible that your goals were too ambitious, or not ambitious enough, or "just right," but you still didn't achieve them. At the beginning of each semester, I recommend that you review and revise your goals. Set new, even higher, goals if you've already achieved the ones you set. If you hit that 3.4 GPA, then shoot for 3.6 for next semester. If you can read 25 pages of a book in an hour, then shoot for 30. The purpose, again, is to keep you focused and motivated, and to stretch your capabilities. By revising your goals upward, you'll be experiencing the fruit of the "growth mindset."

## First Things First: Set Priorities

As you set your goals, you need to be clear about your priorities. Those priorities should take precedence when you set up your schedule. In his book *First Things First*, Steven Covey makes the argument that humans have four basic and essential needs: "To Live, To Love, To Learn, and To Leave a Legacy." He goes on to say that tasks or appointments to fulfill *these* needs or priorities should be the first entries each week in your calendar, even before all of the routine appointments like classes or club meetings. He calls these four highest needs the "Big Rocks." (He's even done demonstrations to show that large rocks have to be loaded into a container before smaller objects like gravel, sand and water; otherwise, there'll be no room for them. Likewise, if you allow your (less-important) routines to fill your schedule, then you won't have time to do what Covey calls "What Matters Most.")

Let's pause for a brief description of each of those "Big Rocks," or priorities, and some thoughts on how you'd incorporate them into your schedule:

- **To Live** addresses your physical needs such as eating, getting adequate sleep, exercising and managing your critical finances. For instance, you should schedule time in your calendar (as your first act each week) to get seven to eight hours of sleep each night (I'll come back to this), when you'll have sit-down meals, when you'll exercise, and if you have a job, when you'd have to go to work. I plan the days on which I'll run, and ensure that late nights be coupled with late mornings to allow for at least seven hours of sleep each night.

- **To Love** speaks to the importance of your relationships. Start with your parents, then move to your siblings. When will you call them? (In this era of smartphones, some college students talk, text and FaceTime with their parents daily. In my opinion, that's too frequent — your parents need to grow up!) If you have close friends, or a boyfriend or girlfriend, schedule times to get together. When are you most likely to hang out with them? Put that in your calendar! You'll be able to relax and enjoy the moment with them if you know that you've planned to have this conversation or hangout with them. They'll sense that they are important when you are truly "present" with them and not worrying about the work you're not getting done. I schedule time to call my mother, who is in her late 80s, at least twice a week.

- **To Learn** speaks to your intellectual engagement. That's what you're doing every day and every week in college, and it's the main purpose of this book. However, you should also consider a skill or two that will help you get *better* at school and at life. Covey calls this "sharpening the saw." In his book, he cites a parable about the man who is seen cutting down a tree with a dull saw. When asked why he doesn't sharpen the saw, the man retorts that he's too busy cutting down the tree. He doesn't realize that if he took the time to sharpen the saw, it would take him less time to cut down the tree! What skills do you need to sharpen? For instance, do you type well? Will developing your typing skill improve your productivity? What about writing? If you sat through a tutorial at the Writing Center on campus as I suggested in Chapter 2, perhaps you can learn to write better and faster. Or maybe it's research in a field that interests you; you'd like to become a more efficient researcher. Whatever skill you decide to sharpen, make it one of your goals for the semester, and schedule time each week to develop it. To sharpen my intellectual saw, I plan time to read books and articles, and listen to podcasts about subjects that interest me. To "chunk" two of my priorities, I listen to podcasts during my weekly long runs.

- **To Leave a Legacy** is your spiritual need. Mr. Covey uses his "Legacy" time to read the Scriptures. I go to church, pray, and read the Scriptures as well. For you, especially if you don't see yourself as religious, you may want to build time into your schedule to meditate, to journal and reflect on your thoughts and aspirations. Regardless of your religious affiliation, Covey says, we all have a yearning to connect with something bigger than ourselves, whether it's a cause, a mission, or a deity — or all of the above. Regardless of what that "something bigger" is for you, schedule time each week to attend to it. For me, taking 10 to 15 minutes each morning to pray for my family, close friends, pastors and coworkers — by name and by need — helps to center me each day and connect with my source of inspiration, wisdom and guidance. While in college, as I do now, I attended weekly services at my local church. In college, I'd go to the early service, which was time-bound by a later service, to ensure that I could get back to campus to study. Making time for these transcendent activities balances your life and adds perspective.

## MANAGING TIME VS. HARNESSING TIME

The third major premise is that the Behavior Shift I'm advocating is not a time-*management* approach. I don't believe anyone can "manage" time. Only one person in recorded history has ever stopped the sun from making its rounds (or technically, stopped the earth from rotating), and the Bible records that "there never been a day like that before or since — God took orders from a human voice" (Joshua 10:14, MSG)! So, since no one other than Joshua has ever been able to cause the earth to stop rotating, you shouldn't expect that *you* can. Time will proceed as designed. But rather than trying to manage it, you can learn to harness it. You can learn to turn it to your own best purposes.

Harnessing time is not an art, but a science. So let me suggest some ways you can effectively harness time — by the semester, by the week, even by the day — and then offer some additional suggestions on how to use time effectively to prepare for exams.

# HARNESSING TIME BY SEMESTER, BY WEEK, AND BY DAY

## SOME GENERAL SUGGESTIONS

Let's start with some overall suggestions. Here are six steps for harnessing time at the beginning of the semester.

1. **Find a calendar or a calendar app that you can use and that will always be with you.**

Your calendar app should not only enable you to easily enter your appointments (classes, assignments due, holidays, etc.) but just as important, you should be able to capture your *to do*s. That is, a list of your tasks and when you will do them (on what day) in order to keep up with your work. I use a cloud-based app called *Todoist* that's linked to my Gmail calendar and accessible across multiple devices including my smartphone. You can use Google Docs or any other app that has both a calendar and "to do" list. When I was in college, deprived of all of these high-tech devices and apps, I used a paper calendar and notebook paper to record my *to do*s." That worked, too. Now, of course, it's even easier. Whatever device-and-app combination works for you, use the first part of the semester to become familiar with it. You don't want to waste time fiddling with its features when you should be focused on your work.

2. **Get enough sleep**

You need seven to eight hours of sleep each night to operate at optimal mental capacity. We often try to shortcut this physical requirement (and end up shortchanging ourselves) by getting less sleep, then drinking coffee, espresso, Red Bull or some other stimulant just to stay awake. When you stay awake past the point where your body would naturally call it a night, you mortgage sleep from the next day, and you'll need even more stimulants to keep you awake the next night. It's a vicious cycle.

Researchers now know that your brain needs adequate sleep time to consolidate all the information it processed during the day. The process of turning this electrical and chemical stimulation into memories is called "encoding." Have you ever struggled with a problem, "slept on it" and, the next morning, found that the solution came to you? Our brains actually encode these connections into our long-term memory while we sleep. In fact, the more complex the material you're learning, the more helpful sleep is in firming up your understanding and enhancing your ability to recall.[16] That's the power of the brain at work.

I tell students that getting a good night's sleep before a significant exam is not only helpful for recall, but it will actually lower their anxiety level as well, since the executive function of their brain, the prefrontal cortex, is most active at thinking and reasoning when they're rested. I found my own thoughts flowed much more fluidly onto paper after I've had a good rest than when I was up all night trying to write the thing! Sometimes it's better to close the computer and get a short nap than to try to plow through. Better still, making those seven to eight hours of sleep per night a regular practice will minimize those all-nighters and crunch periods. In the end, you may find that it'll take less time to do the same work that once required all-nighters. Even if it doesn't, you can be assured that you'll be using that time more effectively: You'll write a better paper or do better on an exam.

### 3.  Eat balanced meals

There is a direct link between your diet and your mental capacity and health. Most college students choose foods that are heavy in saturated fat, sugar and other carbohydrates without balancing them with foods that are known to improve brain function. Researchers have found enough evidence to suggest that proteins such as those found in lean salmon, lean beef, eggs; and other nutrients found in most vegetables such as spinach, can boost recall and improve brain function.[17]

### 4. Avoid carbohydrate overload — it makes you "loopy"

Don't go overboard on carbohydrates — chips, pastries, cookies, candy, and soda. They may fill you up, and even give you a short-term energy boost, but that's all it is: a short-term boost. In fact, you'll soon experience an energy crash that'll bring your energy level down below where you started. Then you're forced to go to sleep or to take a stimulant to keep you awake. My friend used to call that sluggish feeling "loopiness." Being loopy doesn't bring out your best performance.

### 5. Go easy on caffeine, sugar and other mood-swinging foods

I didn't start drinking coffee until my junior year in college. Prior to that, I seemed to get by without it. Once I started, though, I couldn't stop. Coffee and other caffeinated stimulants like Red Bull are addictive in a sinister way. By regularly consuming them, your body constantly craves more. For instance, the more coffee you drink, the more difficult it will be to wake up in the morning — which means you'll need even *more* coffee.

If you already don't drink coffee or other stimulants like Red Bull, stay away from them. If you know what I'm saying because you drink a lot, then try to wean yourself off of them completely, or at least limit how much you drink. I use vacation time to go cold turkey because on vacation, I can usually sleep whenever I want. Then I try to bring that behavior back to my "workday" life.

### 6. Keep your room and your belongings organized

If you have a messy room, it is harder to be efficient in your work. Too much of your time will be spent looking for things, rather than doing what you're supposed to be doing. I tell my freshmen, "*Never keep your room more than five-minutes messy.*" Say you get a call that an unexpected visitor is coming by to see you; you should be able to straighten your room in five minutes. If it'll take you more than that to clean up your papers, put your dirty clothes in a laundry bag or basket, hang up or fold your clean clothes, then it's likely that you're not optimizing your time because your room is messy. More troubling: If you can't find something — an old problem set, the solutions to a problem set, your notes or a textbook — you'll be tempted to slip the assignment or avoid reviewing that material.

An organized room gives you greater control over your domain. Use a file cabinet for important papers. Label manila and hanging folders by subject or club. Use binders with subdividers so sections are clearly organized. Better yet, scan and upload important documents into cloud-based storage systems such as Dropbox, Google Drive, or Apple's iCloud. Either way, whether you choose new-school or old-school methods, or both, by organizing your material, you're ensuring that reference information is easily accessible so you won't have an excuse not to look something up. And who knows, you may impress your visitor!

### 7.  Maximize your periods of peak efficiency

You've probably noticed that your body, and your mind in particular, operate at peak efficiency during certain parts of the day. For me, it's between 4 and 8 p.m. and 4 and 8 a.m. If I'm writing during these periods, words just flow out of my mind onto paper with ease. Catch me between 1 and 3 in the afternoon, however, and the opposite story emerges. I'm dragging, finding it hard to concentrate and stay focused. I write and speak like I'm drowning in molasses. It turns out that our brains cycle through periods of high and low energy called ultradian rhythms. These fluctuations typically last for 90 to 110 minutes according to Eric Jensen.[18]

Do you know when it seems easiest for *you* to focus and learn, and when it's hardest? Those are valuable things to know.

Because of what I know about me, I started scheduling routine work, such as doing my laundry, checking email, or returning phone calls, during my low-energy periods. Whenever possible, I make sure I'm positioned to do my most intellectually challenging work during my peak-efficiency times. That's when I do my heaviest reading, or writing. Find the optimal times that work for you. Experiment with different times of day for various tasks. You'll find your rhythm, and you can start taking advantage of it.

A word of caution: You may not always have the luxury of working when you're at your ultradian best. Your schedule may not allow it. It's important that you learn to discipline yourself to work at any time that your schedule dictates. But to the extent you can balance your work around your own mental rhythms, so much the better.

## HARNESSING TIME BY SEMESTER

You should never stumble into a semester or quarter. Your planning should be intentional. Prior to the beginning of every semester, before classes begin or soon after, take the time to follow these six steps:

1. **Collect all your syllabi**

Every class should have a syllabus, the document the professor distributes or posts at the beginning of class containing the course outline, lecture topics, assignments and their due dates, grading policy, exam schedule, and office hours. If your professor doesn't voluntarily distribute one, ask for it. Collect *and review* all the syllabi for your classes. They'll give you an early — and valuable — overview of your upcoming semester.

2. **Record dates in your planner**

Record all critical dates for each class in your calendar. These should include the dates on which all of your assignments are due — problem sets, papers, and special projects. Also record your exam dates, including midterms and finals. Be as descriptive as possible so you'll recognize the assignment at a glance. In other words, don't just enter "Problem

Set Due" — you won't know which problem set for which course. Rather, enter "CHEM201 Problem Set Due."

I recommend you also enter in your planner key dates for important non-academic appointments or events. For instance, if your student group is going on a retreat, or your fraternity will be conducting a busy recruiting program over a weekend, put those dates in your calendar as well. You don't want to be surprised.

### 3. Identify and anticipate crunch weeks

After you enter all of these dates, step back and review your calendar for each month of the semester. Are there any crunch weeks — weeks in which you have multiple exams and/or problem sets due? Whether your college is on the semester or the quarter system, you'll almost certainly have a crunch week or two by Week Five. If you don't plan for it, you can easily fall behind and never catch up! Once you identify the crunch week, you might want to block out the prior weekend so you can be proactive in using that time to study, to prepare the project, or to write the paper(s). That will be the weekend that you skip the parties or organizational retreats and take up residence in the library!

### 4. Gather all your required reading material

From the syllabus, find out what books and other readings you'll be required to buy (or borrow), and which are optional. If you rely on a campus bookstore, it's important to buy all the required books right away for two reasons. First, you'll be able to purchase your books before the bookstore runs out. Don't wait for the week or day before the reading is due to buy the book; when you need it most, it may no longer be available.

Second, if you go early, you're more likely to save money by finding a used copy of the book or finding it online. Many students sell their books back to the bookstore after a semester, leaving a good inventory of discounted books at the beginning of the next semester. Going early means you'll have a better chance of purchasing a used book and saving yourself some dollars. Of course, searching online for texts may be ideal. The key here is to secure your reading material early.

## 5. Understand course learning objectives and the curriculum plan

When I was in college, I wanted to know the big picture before I got into the minutia of the course material. If I didn't get the big picture, I often didn't get what the course was all about until the midterm or the final, when I had a chance to synthesize the content across multiple weeks or months. Having the overview, on the other hand, was like riding the Sky Train at the amusement park before doing anything else. You get to see the lay of the land, enabling you to map out your strategy for the day.

Getting the big picture helped me understand how concepts or ideas strung together, and helped me anticipate where the professor was going. It turns out that there's some brain science behind this phenomenon. If an overview of a course or subject is introduced first, you're more likely to recall the course material than if you started by being exposed to the parts or the details. Our minds remember things better when we can connect concepts into a "global" understanding. By seeing the big picture, you prime your brain so that when you see the material again, you're more likely to experience that "Aha!" moment. Reviewing the syllabus, discussing the course with the professor early in the semester (as I suggested in the previous chapter), or even reviewing the textbook's Table of Contents are great ways to speed up those "Aha!" moments and increase your recall.[19]

## 6. Form study groups

I've already written about how important study groups are and how to utilize them for maximum impact; my recommendation here is to form these groups at the start of the semester. Reach out to classmates before classes begin, once you have a class schedule and know when your assignments are due.

Again, these are six things you should do before classes even begin for the quarter or semester, or during the first week of classes at the latest. The next section describes ways you can harness time each week.

## HARNESSING TIME BY WEEK

At the beginning of each week, be sure you set your priorities and plan your work for the week ahead. In college, I began doing this on Sunday afternoon. However, I quickly discovered that if I began planning my work for the week on Sunday, I had already fallen behind. The weekend was wasted. The workload was so great early in the week that, if I had begun planning earlier, I would have made better use of the weekend. And so I recommend that you take the following steps on Thursday night, or by Saturday morning at the latest. This way, you can do exactly what you need to do over the weekend to catch up and eventually get ahead of your work.

1. **Define your weekly *First Things First* goals (*To Live, To Love, To Learn, To Leave a Legacy*)**

As I stated earlier, you should begin planning for the week by scheduling your essential priorities, the *Big Rocks* that Stephen Covey described as our essential human needs: to live, love, learn, and leave a legacy. Refer to the previous section for a refresher.

2. **Post your deadlines and study-group schedule on your calendar**

At the beginning of the week (or at the end of the previous one), put all your classes and all your exams and assignments due in the upcoming week into your calendar. Many of these may already be there from the exercise you followed at the start of the semester, but these dates change, and others may have been added to the schedule. Also, plug in your professors' office hours, and any exam reviews that might be scheduled. Finally, plug in your study groups' schedules. Once all these dates are posted, it's time to think about how much prep work is required for each class, exam, paper, or homework assignment, and start blocking out the time to do this work.

### 3. Prepare your daily "To Do" list

It's not important just to know *when* the assignments are due; it's equally important to start planning the work necessary to *do* the assignments. When will you work on your problem sets, research and write that paper, or study for that exam this week? I recommend that you break the tasks up into two-hour blocks so they can be easily scheduled. For instance, if you have a five-page paper to write, then you might separate your tasks into "research topic," "prepare detailed outline," "write first draft," "write final draft."

Place all of your work into your "to do" list. This will be your guide for the week.

Be realistic about the amount of time the work requires. For instance, if a problem set in physics typically takes four hours, then enter the two two-hour blocks when you'll work on it. (And, at the risk of repeating myself, you want to give *yourself* enough time ahead of the due date to review your work with your study group, and to get any questions answered a day or more before the deadline.) If you planned last time for something to take two hours to complete, and it took four, then block off four hours this time. If it turns out to take only two, then you have an extra two hours. However, if you plan for something to take less time and it takes more, it'll push back other work or leave you unprepared in other ways, too. So be realistic.

### 4. Go see your Instructor or TA!!!!

Schedule time to see your instructor and/or teaching assistant each week. If there are scheduled office hours, then plug them into your calendar, even if you don't know what you'll discuss. As I discussed in the Connections Shift chapter, strengthening your relationship with your instructor is essential for learning, but also for maximizing your college experience and your professional and personal development.

## HARNESSING TIME BY DAY

Spend five to ten minutes every day to plan your next day's work. It's best to plan the next day before you go to bed so once again you know how much work you need to do and therefore when you need to wake up. Regardless, though, of whether you plan at night or in the morning, make sure you take the time to plan. Begin by reviewing your *Big Rocks* priority goals for that day. Is this a day you set aside to exercise? Were you able to be true to your sleep goals? What "learn" tasks are you going to employ to "sharpen your saw"?

Then adjust your schedule as necessary. You may have completed an assignment or task sooner than anticipated when you created your plan at the beginning of the week. More likely, though, a problem set, paper or study prep will take longer than you expected. Make the necessary adjustments in your schedule for the day. Move some work around if necessary. In a phrase? Plan ahead, but stay flexible.

### WHAT TO DO *BEFORE* CLASS

**1. Review your last class notes before your next class.**

Most students don't look at their notes until they have to study for a test. I recommend that you review the notes from that course's previous class prior to the next class. Taking 30 minutes or less to go over what was taught last time will enable you to connect new material to concepts you've already learned. That, in turn, will increase your ability to recall and understand this new material. (See the left side of the figure below.) If you skip this step, every lecture or class becomes its own little information island (right side of the figure), and it's much harder to connect the dots and see how everything fits together.

So get into the habit of reviewing your notes. Making additional notes in the margins while you're reviewing them will push you to actively engage with the material and involve more of your brain in the process; that's the path to even more effective learning. Similarly, make note of questions you'll want to ask the professor or TA during "board time," or during class, or both!

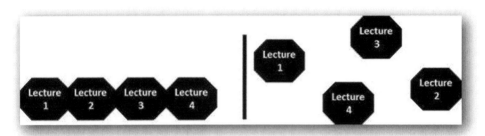

## 2. Do the reading. (Really!)

Second, do the reading assigned for the upcoming class. Yes, I said do the reading. Many students have lost the art of reading before class, particularly if the class is taught in a lecture format and there's no risk of being called upon. You typically don't have that "luxury" in classes when you're expected to participate — say, for a course in modern literature or modern language. But in a lecture course, there's a tendency to avoid doing the reading, or at best, to read the assigned material later, when it comes time to do your homework or study for a test.

What's the problem with that approach? Actually, there are several problems. Here's one: Waiting that long to do the reading increases the likelihood that you'll have to cram, which will reduce your ability to master the subject matter. You do so at your peril.

Here's another: Without reading the material ahead of time, you may very well sit in class and take diligent notes, but you're essentially a robot, relegated to a passive mode of receiving information. And, of course, if you didn't get adequate sleep the night before, your note-taking will be suspect. (See how it all fits together?) So not only will you be seeing the material for the first time, you may not even be able to take accurate notes to review later what you should have started to learn already.

When I was growing up, there used to be prolific series of Public Service Announcements hosted by a nonprofit group, "Reading Is Fundamental," and by the Ad Council, designed to promote literacy among young people. Well, reading *is* fundamental, not just for young children but in college as well! Doing the reading before class is essential for accelerating the rate at which you learn the material. You may not fully understand what you're reading when you see the material for the first time. However, you're "priming" the new material in your brain. When you subsequently sit in lecture, you awaken these "primed" memories and begin to make connections with what you've already read.[20] Thus, sitting in lecture will foster a whole new level of engagement. It's like having a déjà vu experience. You're no longer sitting there passively taking notes. Rather, you're having repeated "Aha!" moments.

Over time, as you keep doing the reading *before* your classes, your previewing skill will improve. Take active notes as you skim the reading. Try connecting this new material to the previous lecture or reading. The more parts of your brain you involve — regions involved with sight (reading), movement (writing), and reasoning (synthesizing new material), the more likely you'll have those "Aha!" moments later.

More importantly, we typically remember new material for only a few seconds if we don't take steps to synthesize it — in other words, to move it to our long-term memory. That's why I encourage you to write as you read, by taking notes in and after each section or page.[21]

## WHAT TO DO *DURING* CLASS

On the day of class, show up a few minutes early. Greet the professor or TA and use the "board time" if needed as I noted earlier.

### 1. Sit front and center

Sit in a location that will receive most of the instructor's visual attention, which is usually front and center. (In a lecture hall, it may be a few rows up from the first row, at eye level.) That will assure that the instructor sees you. Good professors will constantly check the faces of the students to gauge their reaction to the material being presented. If yours is the face the professor sees most often, your responses are most likely to govern the pace, and even the direction, of the lecture.

At the front-and-center position, you'll also be seen most frequently when you signal that you have a question. In addition, by having a significant amount of the "air time," your professor will gradually associate you with being a good and strong student. This may come in handy during grading!

Sitting front and center also forces you to stay alert. If you've taken my advice and done the reading, then it's more likely you will be engaged. The instructor will see that engagement in your facial expressions, note-taking, and questions you raise. On the other hand, dozing off while sitting front and center will damage the impression the professor or TA has of you. So it's important to stay alert, even if you have to force yourself to do it. Take a break and go splash water on your face. Chew gum. Whatever it takes, don't fall asleep. If nothing works, then don't sit there. You'll be hurt more by falling asleep in the instructor's face than by sitting in the back of the class this one time.

## 2. Take *useful* notes

Some educators recommend a variety of note-taking techniques. The Cornell method is the most popular model (see below).[22]

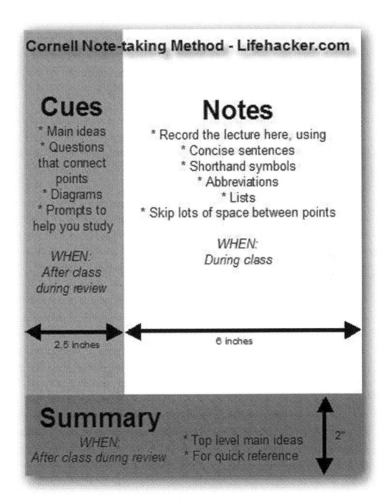

The Cornell system recommends that you divide up your page and take in-class notes in the "Notes" section that occupies about 2/3 of the page. Don't write down every word your professor says, but instead use concise sentences, symbols, and abbreviations to capture the core of it. While you're writing, constantly ask yourself about the meaning of the material you're being taught. Keep a dialogue going in your head. How does this theory or concept square with your reading? Is the professor emphasizing a point that you really need to remember later? The key here, again, is not to be just a passive recipient of information, but to intellectually engage yourself in the process. This approach assures that you're *actively* engaged in the learning process. You don't want to be that robot, right?

So your in-class notes have filled about 2/3 of each page. Now use the remaining areas for "Cues." Use "Cues" to write down questions you can ask your professor, TA or study-group partners either during or after class. That will make it easier to review, and understand, the material later on.

I didn't use the Cornell system as an undergraduate or graduate student. I just wrote everything that appeared on the board in my notebook, which was *not* the most efficient and effective approach. If I had a question, though, I would write it in the margins. The Cornell system would have been a great improvement for me, and it may be just the thing for you. The key is to experiment with multiple techniques early in the semester until you find the approach that best meets your needs.

### 3. Avoid distractions

If you take notes on a laptop or tablet and have a tendency to get distracted — surfing the web, browsing Instagram, answering instant messages, or checking your Twitter feeds — then close the laptop, turn off the iPad, and take notes the old-fashioned way. And put your phone away (unless you're using the camera or the voice recorder to take notes.) Texting or taking a call in class is the best way to learn nothing — and to piss off the professor while you're at it. If for some reason you *have* to text, don't do it from the "front and center" seats. If you're sitting there, excuse yourself, go out in the hall, take care of your business, and get back to learning.

## WHAT TO DO *AFTER* CLASS

### 1. Get answers to the "Cues" section notes.

Immediately after class, ask the professor or TA the questions you've noted in your "Cues" section. *Write down the answers.* You may not have time for a follow-up question, so make sure you capture what is being said.

## 2.  Summarize your notes

As soon as you leave the classroom — or within no more than a few hours, as your schedule allows — review your notes while they're still fresh. (I used to do this over lunch or during breaks.) Find a quiet space or a location like a library or reading room, where you won't be bothered. Take 15 to 30 minutes to fill in the gaps in your notes.

Reviewing the material immediately after class "activates" your mind and strengthens your memories. As one researcher put it, "What is reviewed is remembered."[23]

Here is when the Cornell system really comes in handy. After you've reviewed the "Notes" section to fill in the gaps in your note-taking, use the left side of the page (the "Cues" section) to note the broad concepts being taught. Think of them as section headings. "Rotational energy." "Derivatives." "Shakespearean connections."

Now, on the bottom of the page in the "Summary" section, summarize your notes, again in your own words. This forces you to synthesize the material and helps to solidify your learning. It also helps your ability to remember the material because you are "chunking," or grouping, the material in an easier-to-remember format. Finally, by taking the time to note your questions, and summarizing and synthesizing concepts, you'll make your review for homework and exam preparation much easier.

## 3.  Start your homework early

Start your homework on the day it's given, even if the material has not yet been covered in class. By doing so, you are effectively previewing new material, which increases your engagement in class. You'll find yourself saying, "Oh, that's what the homework means by..." (You might even have used class time or "board time" to ask questions about the homework — without being too obvious, of course.) I'd recommend taking 30 minutes to an hour each day to work on your assignment, particularly after the material is covered in the readings and the lecture, rather than trying to cram it all in the night before it's due.

### 4. Discuss the lecture

If you have a chance, it will be very helpful to discuss the lecture with others. Here is where a study group would be most valuable, as we discussed in the *Connections Shift* chapter. But even outside of a formal study group, you can do this over lunch or dinner. Occasionally, my friends and I would get together for lunch after physics class and make jokes about the material. (Not about the professor.) While our jokes were harsh and, admittedly, very nerdy — remember the "relativity" joke about the way somebody's girlfriend would look after she traveled nearly the speed of light? — what we didn't know at the time that we were solidifying our understanding of the material. But you know it now. So think of conversation (even, at times, *silly* conversation) as another learning tool.

Whatever your method, whether in study groups, Socratic circles, or joking over meals, if you have the chance to discuss material with others while it's still fresh, take advantage of the opportunity.

### 5. Turn your assignments in on time

Finally, make sure you turn your homework in on time! Since a significant percentage of your grade is based on your assignments, it behooves you not to be late. In fact, why let yourself lose points for this? It's a no-brainer, particularly if you plan your work each week and utilize your study group, and you begin working on your assignments the day they're assigned. There should be no excuses for missing assignment deadlines. None.

## PREPARING FOR EXAMS

Back in Chapter 1, I shared with you how I discovered *The Deep Dive Learning Approach*. This section will provide a step-by-step approach for preparing for exams, and some of the rationale behind it as well. While this approach will mostly benefit those taking quantitative courses, the principles I discuss here also apply to less computational exams — for example, those in English, history, or sociology. No matter what the subject is, consider my exam-prep suggestions this way: "Eat the meat and spit out the bones." In other words, try this process, but ultimately your goal will be to find the approach that works for you and your particular learning style. Ready? Here we go!

### 1. Find a Location to Go Deep

As noted, find a location that you'll use for studying. This should be a quiet place where you can concentrate, one to which you can return throughout the semester, and indeed throughout your college career. Studies show that physical settings influence what and how you hear, feel, and see, and these senses in turn influence your mental performance and emotional state.[24]

To the degree possible, the place you choose should match the test environment in terms of the noise level and, if possible, even the seating; you don't want your exam space to feel totally unfamiliar. Think of a drama troupe preparing for their performance. A few nights before Opening Night, they hold rehearsals on the very stage on which they'll be performing. You're effectively doing the same thing, "rehearsing the learning," as Dr. Jensen states. That way, you won't have to deal with new emotions — the anxiety caused by unfamiliarity — at exam time, the very time your brain needs to turn in its peak cognitive performance.

Now, what else should happen?

### 2. Schedule Your Study Group for Exam Prep

It won't *happen* first, but you may want to *schedule* first, or at least well in advance: Make sure you've set a time closer to the exam for your study group to get together to test each other. This may be your regular study group, or an ad hoc group of friends and classmates whose purpose is to come together for exam prep. Optimally, you would want to meet the night before the exam to test each other after you've all had the chance to study individually. That way, time won't be wasted on absorbing the concepts; you'll be presenting them, and testing each other on the facts, procedures, or ideas the exam will be assessing. As we've discussed earlier — remember the "sandwich"? — preparing on your own first, and only then getting together with your classmates, and then back to solo work, is the best use of your time and theirs. But you still have to schedule a time for your group to get together. Do it in advance.

Now that you know the importance of finding the right *place* for you to study for exams, and you've scheduled your study group, let me turn to *how* to study for them.

## WHAT TO DO TWO DAYS BEFORE THE EXAM

Two (or more) days before your exam, your exam prep should be dedicated to understanding the concepts, theories, ideas and procedures that will be tested. Giving yourself at least two days gives you time to internalize the material, enabling your brain to migrate information to your long-term memory. You also avoid cramming, which has the opposite effect, because of the stress associated with working at the last minute, and the limited time you've allowed yourself to try to synthesize the materials. Not enough synthesis results in very short-term retention — it's here today and gone when you need to recall it.

Set aside sufficient time to review all of the readings and lecture notes. Here, the Cornell note-taking method will be helpful because you will have summarized the notes in your own language after every lecture. I was, and still am, a line-by-line reader, and so I would plan to spend four to six hours combing through the materials. If I started after dinner — say, at 6 p.m. — I'd wrap up at about midnight, with two breaks. Your own review may take just as long, or possibly longer, depending on how much you'll have to cover, and how fast you read. If that seems intense to you, it is. But that's the focus and dedication required to master the material and be successful in college.

Should you break up the time into less than two-hour blocks or less than four to six hours? If you have to, yes. (You may need to start an hour at a time, but work your way up to studying in two-hour blocks.) However, I would discourage it. It's harder for you to get restarted, and to maintain your momentum, if you break up your "deep dive" learning. That's why TV writers often feel the need to start each new episode with "Previously…" — they can't count on you to remember the key details from last time! If you have to, follow their approach, and take some time at the beginning of your "next episode" to review your notes from the previous one.

If you can't schedule four to six hours to study two days before the exam, then block off the time *three* days before the exam. Never give yourself only one day, the day before the exam, to start this process. You won't have enough time to absorb the material. Nor will you have time to get those remaining questions answered by your professor or TA.

Now, I recognize that there will be times during your college career when you won't have the luxury of starting your preparation two or more days before an exam. (In a moment, I'll share a shortcut with you.) However, a short prep time should be the exception, not the rule.

## 1. Gather Your Study Aids

Prior to going to your study location, two (or more) days before the exam, gather all of the materials you'll need to study — textbooks/readings, notebooks, graded assignments, problem sets and exams from previous years that you can get my hands on. Bring a separate notebook or notepad app to capture your notes before each exam. You'll ultimately reference them for the final exam.

## 2. Comb Through Your Readings and Notes

Actively review all of the readings by writing notes as you go, as we discussed earlier. The more parts of your brain you use, the more you'll recall. By reading, seeking to understand, *and* writing you're making neural connections that are more lasting than if you merely read — or, even worse, just browsed. You'll also help transfer your knowledge from short-term to long-term memory.

As you read, write down key definitions, concepts, ideas and procedures in your dedicated notebook or app. Jot down theories and definitions that are hard to understand and that you'll need for later review. Note questions that you'll ask your TA or one of your classmates the next day. Work the problems as they appear in the text, once again, in your notebook. Try working them on your own before referring to the steps and solutions that are in the text. If you get stuck, check the text for the next steps, then try to continue on your own.

Jot down the explanations as well, in your own words. Here, you're attempting to understand the "Why," not just to memorize the "What," for each step in the procedure. A good professor will test you on the "Why?" (and not just have you regurgitate procedures from memory) by giving you a problem that might look completely unfamiliar to you, but that forces you to think about, and then apply, the concepts you've learned. (Or haven't.)

I recall the physics instructor for my summer bridge program in college had an obsession with the movie *Star Wars*. (He actually reminded us of Darth Vader by the way he wore his hair.) For his exams, we had to determine distance and collision points between Luke Skywalker's Starfighter and Darth Vader's TIE fighter. The setup to the problem was completely "alien" to us. (Sorry!) He had not used the *Star Wars* context for his lectures or problem sets, but he did so in the exams. After we got over the initial surprise, though, the underlying principles of mechanics carried us through. A good professor will give you the tools to solve problems even in novel contexts. If you've studied the concepts, and not just the procedures, then you'll be prepared to take on anything, including the Death Star!

### 3. Take Regular Breaks

Give yourself breaks every 90 minutes to two hours. The long periods of studying between breaks will force you to focus and absorb what you're learning. The short breaks, in turn, will help you stay sharp during those periods of focused review. Like working out, learning improves with focused sessions and resting intervals rather than with constant exposure to new material. If you're not used to sitting still for two hours at a time, then work your way up to it, as I suggested earlier. Start with whatever block of time works for you but is still long enough to make you study in a concentrated way. Even if it's 30 minutes, stay focused for that 30 minutes, then get up and walk around. After two hours, have a light snack such as a piece of fruit or some nuts. Stick with snacks that will help get your blood flowing to your brain, but won't make you sleepy later, as a piece of candy or a sweet pastry would.

If you've followed these suggestions, you should find you've increased your understanding and your retention of the material, as well as your ability to apply what you've learned in a variety of contexts.

You're now ready to make the final push the day before the exam.

## The Day Before the Exam

Make sure you get your questions answered that arose during your review the day or evening before. Seek out your TA or an informed classmate to discuss any lingering confusion. Since most course material builds on previous knowledge, a gap in your understanding may limit your grasp of more complex content. So it's important to get answers and gain complete understanding — leave no knowledge behind!

### 1. Gather Your Study Aids Again

Get ready to study by gathering all of the materials you had the night before. It is said that *prior planning prevents poor performance*. The more you plan, the better your performance and, in this case, the less likely you'll have to interrupt your study to go back to your dorm to get something. You don't want to give yourself excuses.

### 2. Back on Your Own

You've returned to your "deep dive" study location. You've even managed to secure one of the same spots you've used previously, so you don't have to spend any time getting used to it, figuring out where the plugs or the bathrooms are, etc. At this critical point, you want a familiar location, someplace that will spur you to get right to work.

### 3. Review Notes from the First Night of Study, Then Work Problems

While the previous day of solo study — the first layer of the "sandwich" — was dedicated to understanding concepts, this second day should be dedicated to applying those concepts — that is, to problem solving.

Begin by reviewing the material you recorded the night before in your dedicated notebook. Review the sample problems; again, make sure you understand the "Whys," not just the "What's?" After your review, begin working problems. Begin by redoing the problems in the textbook. See if you can do them on your own. If not — but only when you get stuck — then refer to your text. Understand what the next steps are, then turn over your notes and continue working the problem. Like actors practicing their lines in a play, focus on the areas you're having difficulty mastering. When you're done, do it again, until you've locked it in.

After you've worked the problems in your notebook from the previous night's text reading, follow the same approach and start working the problems from your lecture notes. Try working the problems on your own, and keep a running dialogue in your head: "How did she do that?" "Why did he go to this step?" Again, refer to your notes only if you get stuck, and then rework the problem without the notes.

Next, turn to your old problem sets that cover the material that will be on the test. Don't just look over the problem sets: Work those problems. Work each problem as if you're in the exam. If you get stuck, refer to the solution sets only to understand the next step. If you haven't worked the problem cleanly, without errors, do it again until you get it right.

It's a lot of work, yes? Yes. But as you begin to work the volumes of problems in the sequence I'm suggesting — and you're taking appropriate breaks and eating the right kinds of snacks, right? — you'll notice that you're developing a problem-solving rhythm. Every problem has a rhythm, an approach, and you're learning how to tap into that rhythm.

Finally, if you have an old exam given to you by an upperclassman, work the problems in the exam, as if you're taking the exam in real life. See if you can finish it in the same amount of time that is allocated for your exam the next day. If you get stuck, do what you can, then move to the next problem.

After finishing the test, go over the problems that were the most difficult. Review the answer (solution set) and then check your work. If it's correct, then repeat with the next problem, and so on. If you were unable to finish a problem, then go to the solution set to understand what stumped you. Again, ask yourself the why questions — why this step over another? Once you get through that problem, then redo it without help. Always finish the problem without aid from the solution set or your notes. You are synthesizing the material by fostering your own understanding.

Once you've mastered the approach, once you've established that problem-solving *rhythm*, your brain cells are "freed up" to focus on actually solving the problems themselves. Like becoming proficient at riding a bicycle or driving a car, the mechanics of steering, accelerating, braking, and following the rules of the road become practically automated. You simply focus on your destination. Similarly, by practicing your problem solving, you automate your approach and can focus instead on your "destination," the problem you need to solve.

### 4. Review with Your Study Group

Having prepared individually, now would be a good time to get with your study group. This gathering would have been scheduled with a defined start and end time. Two hours is reasonable to get together to test each other, like the students did in the Uri Treisman study. The length of time, though, would depend on the course and the amount of material that needs to be covered.

### 5. Get Some Sleep

The night before the exam, make sure you schedule at least seven hours of sleep. As I've mentioned, you need at least this amount of time for ideas to be consolidated in and by your brain, and transferred from short-term to long-term memory. This, in turn, ensures that you'll make the more lasting neural connections that facilitate recall and understanding. Sleep deprivation puts at risk your ability to remember the material and think creatively, both of which are critical for exams. Why would you do all that prep work and then undermine your efforts by not being at your best? Get your rest, and show them what you've got!

## WORKING SMARTER TAKEAWAYS: THE BEHAVIOR SHIFT

- Set S.M.A.R.T. Goals at the beginning of the semester both for the semester and for your time in college;
- Share your goals with others;
- Revisit and revise your goals;
- Prioritize your basic needs — "To Live," "To Love," "To Learn," "To Leave a Legacy" — and schedule them first in your weekly calendar;
- Harness your time by the semester, by the week, and by the day;
- Prepare for class, take *active* notes during class, and start your homework as soon as possible after class.

## Studying for Exams

- Find a location where you can repeatedly study uninterrupted and that mimics the exam environment;
- Schedule your exam-prep study group ahead of time;
- Two (or more) days before the exam, make sure you understand the concepts;
- One (or more) days before the exam, focus on problem-solving;
- Get sufficient sleep.

# CHAPTER 5

# FINAL THOUGHTS: EMBRACE THE HILLS

ABOUT 10 YEARS ago, I began to ride my bicycle as a way to get in shape and stay healthy. As a college student, I had ridden a bike everywhere — to classes, social events, and even to church — and at any time, through rain and snowstorms, so picking up cycling again was not too much of a stretch for me. I set distance goals that eventually enabled me to ride 70 miles at a stretch. I don't ride as much as I used to because I run now. But occasionally I still take the bike out for a long ride.

During the period when I was working my way up to longer distances, I noticed that I'd avoided a certain route that started with a relatively long uphill climb. Without thinking too much about it, I found myself choosing a less challenging route each time I rode. It turns out that that less challenging route also was less appealing. It was more industrial and less residential and bucolic than the route that began with the hill. The hill route, by contrast, led to some of the best, most picturesque bike routes in the area.

One day, I realized why I was instinctively avoiding this route: It was that hill. Now, this hill wasn't especially formidable. It was about a half a mile long and had a grade of about seven percent, enough to take your breath away, but hardly the French Alps. And yet, because it was at the beginning of the ride, before I was warmed up, I avoided it, and relegated myself to a less-than-satisfying workout. I allowed my fear of hills to preclude me from taking full advantage of these great rides.

I finally decided one morning that I had to embrace the hill.

On that morning, I told myself that I would ride just that one hill, the discouraging one nearest my home, and nothing more. I had, finally, fully embraced the Growth Mindset that Carol Dweck had written about: I believed that I could get better at climbing hills. To that end, I decided to time my progress on my stopwatch, and record how long it would take to ride all the way up the hill, and at what speed. That time, and that speed, would be my benchmarks. I knew I would get better, but I needed a baseline to compare with my future climbs. It also helped me to take my mind off the pain!

I must have ridden that hill 10 times. I rode it different ways — sitting on the saddle, then stomping on the pedals while standing, each time trying to beat my previous time. The reward for working hard was turning around and coasting downhill, reaching speeds of 30 miles an hour with the wind in my face and the joy of knowing I had earned this simple pleasure.

After about 20 minutes of riding up and back down, something happened. I experienced an *Attitude Shift*. My hill-phobia became a hill-affinity. I started to see each hill in front of me as a challenge to be conquered, rather than an obstacle to be avoided. I immediately sought out hills that were more and more challenging. There was one about three miles from my house, about a mile long with a steeper grade than the smaller one near my house. I would ride to that hill and take it repeatedly, once again timing myself so I could measure my progress. I found I actually enjoyed riding hills!

Something else happened as well as I took on longer and steeper routes. That first hill — which I once thought was such a formidable foe — was no longer a challenge for me. For many years that followed, whenever I climbed that hill, I marveled at how I had once feared and viscerally avoided it, rather than embracing it, and embracing the challenge to conquer it.

And it even occurred to me along the way that the hill was a metaphor for another fear I faced up to years earlier. I never considered speaking and writing my "core competencies." When I had to give a speech in church, or a talk at work, I'd have to work very hard at practicing the talk over and over, making sure I got all the transitions right. I drilled myself to ensure I knew exactly what I was going to say, and when and how I would say it. Fear of failure motivated me. I was afraid of experiencing stage fright: Getting up there and not remembering what I was to say or, even worse, having an anxiety attack when all those eyes were on me.

If you saw me at a speaking event today, you'd be thoroughly surprised to hear that I once had this deep fear of speaking — and, for that matter, a resistance to writing, too. After all, over the course of my career, I had given talks to both small and large groups in many different venues. However, my lack of confidence wasn't on display in the speeches or writing assignments I chose to accept. No, it played out in the numerous opportunities I *rejected*, especially on those occasions when I was asked to speak extemporaneously — say, in a workshop or some other informal venue. In those situations, my fears overcame me and I rarely volunteered to be the spokesperson for the group. I simply lacked confidence in these skills. Speaking (and writing) were my hills.

One day, I decided to tackle them the same way I'd taken on that first hill near my house. I resolved that I would no longer avoid situations when I would be called upon to speak. My *growth mindset* instinct kicked in. I resolved to get better at these things. I *needed* to get better if I was to progress in my career as a professional and as a person, so I decided to embrace the challenge.

It was liberating. I made a commitment to volunteer to be the group spokesperson in any class, workshop, or seminar where the opportunity arose, regardless of the status of the other people in the room. Knowing that I wouldn't get it right immediately, I was comfortable with the fact that the first few times I would probably stumble. And I did. I'd forget some things, or bumble through my talking points. Once in a class, I even had an anxiety attack, barely getting through my 10-minute presentation. Still, I leaned in on the growth mindset. I knew that I would get better at it. And I did. (The same with writing projects.)

My attitude about these and other areas of growth now is: "I'm not good at this...*yet*."

I hear countless stories from students about their own fears about math or writing. "I hate math" or "I have problems writing papers" are constant refrains. Students avoid classes, topics, or even majors just to steer clear of doing what they fear most, and professionals decline new assignments. I recently heard about a freshman who chose to switch majors simply to avoid taking chemistry because, six weeks into the semester, he struggled with it. This young man failed to embrace his hill. Too bad.

What's *your* hill?

What subject, assignment or skill do you avoid because you are ostensibly not good at it? Stop and think for a minute. What would happen to your self-esteem, to your quality of life, if you no longer feared that hill? Are there new opportunities that would open up for you if you no longer avoided the scary stuff, but instead embraced the challenge?

Perhaps you can see yourself as a lawyer or teacher after overcoming a fear of public speaking, or an author or professor after committing to developing your writing or analytical skills. Your aspirations aren't quite as grand as these? That's OK. How about no longer being shy around certain people, or getting over the fear of letting your team down at critical moments? Instead, approach that person you've been fearing. Ask for the ball. Take the last shot. You may stumble at first, but commit yourself to getting better. The sky's the limit once you embrace your hill.

You'll need to change the way you do some things, and even the way you think about some things. But as I hope I've made clear, the rewards of making those changes — those shifts — are substantial.

⌒

The Attitude Shift is the first of three shifts you have to make to be successful in college, and in life. As I wrote at the start of our conversation, going to college — and, for that matter, any major transition you tackle after that — is a lot like driving on the highway the first time. It may be scary, but you have to shift gears or you'll be left behind. The Attitude Shift is your critical first step.

Then, you have to step up and start reaching out to faculty, to administrators, your managers and to your peers. The Connections Shift is another opportunity to face your fears and embrace your hills. You may need to overcome shyness or cultural barriers to approaching people in authority or joining a study group. Embrace the hill and commit to getting better at making this outreach. By leveraging your connections on campus, you'll become a better student and a better person, and you'll develop relationships that can last a lifetime.

And finally, as you develop that growth mindset, and the confidence in yourself and your abilities; and as you make connections with faculty, administrators and fellow students, you'll also be making The Behavior Shift to learn how to work smarter. You can't manage time, but you can harness it. And by harnessing time by the semester, by the week, and by day, and by more effectively preparing for exams using *The Deep Dive Learning Approach*, you'll establish the habits of mind that will help you get over your hills.

Do these three shifts *guarantee* success? No. There are no guarantees in life. But I'm confident that if you make these shifts — in your attitude, your connections, and your behavior — you'll become a better student. A better professional. And isn't that what you want? If so, then embrace your hills, and reach for the sky!

I know you can do it.

# ENDNOTES

1    Jensen, E. (2005). *Teaching With the Brain in Mind.* (2nd ed.). Alexandria, VA: Association for Supervision.

2    Dweck, C. (2006). *Mindset: The New Psychology of Success.* New York, NY: Random House, p. 23.

3    Ibid. p. 24.

4    Ibid, p. 33.

5    Ibid, p. 77.

6    Ibid. p. 78.

7    Ibid, p. 77.

8    Ibid, p. 53.

9    Arum, R. & Roksa, J. (2010). *Academically Adrift: Limited Learning on College Campuses.* Chicago, IL: University of Chicago Press, p. 93.

10   Ecclesiastes 4:9

11    LaVant, B.D., Anderson, J.L., & Tiggs, J.W. (2002). Retaining African American Men Though Mentoring Initiatives. *New Directions in Student Services, Winter 1997*(80) 43-53.

12    http://vccslitonline.cc.va.us/mrcte/treisman.htm

13    Arum & Rokso, p. 133.

14    Ibid, p. 100.

15    Meyer, Paul j (2003). "What would you do if you knew you couldn't fail? Creating S.M.A.R.T. Goals" *Attitude Is Everything If You Want to Succeed Above and Beyond.* The Meyer Resource Group, Incorporated.

16    Jensen, p. 130.

17    Ibid, p. 139.

18    Ibid, p. 49.

19    Ibid, p. 142.

20    Ibid, p. 140.

21    Ibid, p. 132.

22    http://homeworkhelpblog.com/the-cornell-note-taking-system/

23    Jenson, pp. 41, 138.

24    Ibid, p. 82.

# APPENDIX

REPRINTED WITH PERMISSION from *The Journal of Negro Education*, 2013, Vol. 82, No.1

## Understanding the Relationships among Racial Identity, Self-Efficacy, Institutional Integration and Academic Achievement of Black Males Attending Research Universities

### Karl W. Reid

*This study asserts that African American males with higher grade point averages (GPAs) in college are also academically and socially integrated into campus and hold racial identity attitudes and self-efficacy beliefs that facilitate their level of institutional integration. The statistical study of 190 African American males attending five research universities reveals that successful African American males report a heightened sense of self-efficacy and were more satisfied with opportunities to interact with faculty. Black males with higher GPAs in college also report higher levels of faculty and social integration, though the relationship is moderated by their racial identity attitudes. Recommendations for improving educational outcomes of Black males attending predominantly White research universities are made.*

***Keywords:*** *Black males, college, achievement*

## INTRODUCTION

African American college-going rates have been on the rise since the late 1960s (Brubacher & Rudy, 2003). This enrollment progress, however, masks a troubling trend in American higher education. According to the U.S. Department of Education's Integrated Postsecondary Education Data System (IPEDS, U.S. Department of Education, 2010a, 2010b) data, African American males make up just 36 percent of all Blacks enrolled in higher education, and only four percent of the total college enrollment. More disturbing is the gap between the bachelor's degrees awarded to African American males and females, a development that began nearly 40 years ago ("Special Report: College Degree Awards," 1999). Black women earned 66 percent of all bachelor's degrees conferred to African Americans in 2008-2009 and a substantial majority of all master's and non-professional doctoral degrees (U.S. Department of Education, 2009).

Contributing to the degree gap is the disproportionate percentage of Black males who fail to complete their postsecondary education. Only 33 percent of African American men attending four-year institutions graduated in six years—the lowest of all population segments—compared to 44 percent of Black women, and 57 percent of White males (U.S. Department of Education, 2010). The graduation gap between Black males and females is the largest gender gap of any subpopulation.

Researchers have proffered disparate theories to explain the low collegiate achievement and high attrition of Black males, including societal discrimination ("Special Report: College Degree Awards," 1999; Wilson, 1996); inadequate pre-college preparation (Cuyjet, 1997; Gainen, 1995; May, 2002; Palmer et al., 2010); financial constraints (Cuyjet, 1997); cultural factors (Coleman et al.,1966; Ogbu, 1990) and genetic deficits (Coleman et al., 1966; Herrnstein & Murray, 1994). However, these suppositions neglect the role of institutional factors within colleges and universities in patterns of underachievement. A few seminal studies about persistence suggest that certain in-college factors may exert a greater influence on collegiate achievement than precollege variables

(Astin, 1993; Bowen & Bok, 1998; Bowen, Chingos & McPherson, 2009; Pascarella & Terenzini, 1991).Tinto (1993) and others (Brown, 1995; Davis, 1994; Johnson, 1993; Palmer & Gasman, 2008; Strayhorn, 2008, 2010) maintained that students, especially Black males who perceive high levels of institutional support, faculty contact, and peer cohesion and congruence with the mainstream of campus life are more likely to graduate. However, little is known about whether the same factors influence the achievement or cumulative grade point average (GPA, not just persistence) of Black males in predominantly White institutions (PWIs) where the majority of Black males are enrolled (Baker, 2007; Knapp, Kelly-Reid, & Whitmore, 2006; Strayhorn, 2010). Furthermore, one knows far less about possible motivational and psychosocial processes that may foster or hinder their campus integration.

This study extends Tinto's (1993) argument that in-college perceptions and experiences may interact with personal attributes and attitudes to moderate levels of institutional integration. By naming the "personal attributes and attitudes," it makes the case that perceived self-efficacy and racial identity attitudes cause African American males to idiosyncratically foster or inhibit their integration into the institutional milieu. Finally, by overlaying three theoretical frames: (a) persistence, (b) self-efficacy, and (c) racial identity it aims to introduce a comprehensive explanation for the achievement of the most successful Black males in college, rather than a simplistic focus on persistence which Tinto's study explicates.

## BACKGROUND LITERATURE

Three bodies of literature have emerged to explain many of the institutional, psychological, and social factors that contribute to African American male underachievement are reviewed in the following section. The persistence literature essentially argues that academic success in college rests on the ability of the student to adjust to, and integrate into the institution both socially and academically (Bonner & Bailey,

2006; Jones, 2001; Moore, 2001; Tinto, 1993). The self-efficacy literature contends that students will be motivated to act and persevere through challenges and to employ effective learning strategies when they believe their actions will produce positive outcomes (Bandura et al., 2001). Finally, there is growing evidence to suggest African Americans attending PWIs may perceive and respond to their academic pursuits and university policies and practices in ways that are influenced by their attitudes toward their individual or reference group identity (Hrabowski, Maton, & Greif, 1998; Johnson, 1993; Noguera, 2003; O'Connor, 1997; Perry, Steele, & Hilliard, 2003; Saunders, 1998).

## PERSISTENCE

In-college experiences have been found to be influential in explaining college student persistence than pre-college factors such as high school grades and test scores (Donovan, 1984). The persistence literature essentially argues that academic success in college rests on the ability of a student to adjust both socially and academically to the institution (Jones, 2001; Moore, 2001; Tinto, 1993). Students who feel that there is an institutional fit—that is, when they become more integrated, involved, and satisfied with the academic and social systems and congruent with the mainstream of campus life—are more likely to graduate (Brown, 1995; Light, 2001; Pascarella & Terenzini, 1991). Institutional fit is predicated on the success with which a student interacts with faculty (academic integration) and students (social integration) because both entities shape the cultural climate of an institution (Tinto, 1993).

**Academic integration: Faculty relationships**. While frequent faculty interactions have empirically proven to benefit all students, faculty expectations (as perceived by the student) have a specifically strong positive influence on the academic outcomes of African American students (Strayhorn, 2010). For instance, Allen's (1992) comparative study of Black students attending historically Black colleges and universities (HBCUs) and PWIs found that perceived level of faculty encouragement had a greater influence on achievement than the racial composition of the institution. Numerous other studies highlight the distinctive ethos of HBCU faculty to foster a sense of belonging and an ethic of care that in turn spur achievement in African American males (Palmer & Gasman, 2008; Palmer & Young, 2009). In a retrospective study of 4,597 students conducted nine years after graduation, personally knowing a faculty member or administrator had a greater effect on educational attainment, occupational status, and annual income for Black men than it did for Black women in the study (Pascarella et al., 1987). Therefore, adult interactions on campus matter for Black males on measures of achievement and college satisfaction (Davis, 1994; LaVant, Anderson, & Tiggs, 1997; Strayhorn, 2008; Thile & Matt, 1995). Social integration also has an effect on persistence.

**Social integration: Peer cohesion.** Successful students are more likely to be involved in college- and student-sponsored events (Pascarella & Terenzini, 1991), and this positive association between social and leadership involvement and achievement holds for Black students at PWIs as well (Baker, 2007; Leppel, 2002; Strayhorn, 2010). For Black males, campus involvement has a stronger positive effect on graduation rate than for White students and Black females, and contributes twice as much to degree completion than do measures of academic integration (Pascarella, 1985). Insight into the specific type of social integration that matters for Black males was revealed by Baker (2008), Pascarella (1985) and others (Harper, 2006; Strayhorn, 2010; Sutton & Terrell, 1997). For instance, serving on a university or departmental committee that sets institutional policy (Pascarella, 1985) and participating in political organizations (Baker, 2008) had the strongest significant influences on degree completion and academic achievement, respectively. More broadly, Harper (2006) discovered that leadership in clubs and organizations were associated with above-3.0 GPA African American males in college.

It is still unclear, however, why some Black males are successful at becoming embedded in the campus life of their PWI and others do not.

If Tinto's (1993) earlier argument is correct, then institutional factors outlined above may interact with personal attributes and attitudes to explain the difference. Such interactions could thereby influence the performance of some more than others. To offer plausible explanations for variations in levels of institutional integration, cognitive and psychosocial perspectives must be considered.

## SELF-EFFICACY

Bandura (1997) maintains that a person's belief about one's expectations and capabilities influences future-oriented behaviors within that domain, and in turn produces outcomes that self-fulfill beliefs. Bandura called this self-fulfilling human agency *self-efficacy*, which is the belief about one's capability to organize and execute courses of action that produce desired performances.

Self-efficacy beliefs have been positively linked to academic achievement, performance expectancies, self-perceptions of competence (Hackett et al., 1992; Stipek, 1984) and possessing positive attitudes toward subject matter (Bandura, 1997). Students with a heightened sense of self-efficacy also tend to take more challenging courses (Eccles, 1994), are better at solving conceptual problems, persist in searching for solutions, and demonstrate better time management (Bandura, 1997).

Self-efficacy beliefs are acquired from four main sources: (a) progressive performance accomplishments (i.e., academic success); (b) vicarious experiences (role models); (c) verbal messages and social persuasions that affirm one's capabilities in the domain or at the task; and (d) physiological states (i.e., anxiety, stress, fatigue, and moodiness), all of which can raise or lower one's self-efficacy (Pajares, 2002).

Although generally informative, these studies offer little insight into the specific effects of self-efficacy on achievement specifically for African American males, though we can draw an inference by juxtaposing three suppositions that stand on reasonably sound empirical grounds. First, studies consistently report lower self-efficacy among racial minority undergraduates, including Black males (Brower &

Ketterhageng, 2004; Combs, 2001; Cuyjet, 1997; Laar, 2000; Mayo & Christenfeld, 1999). Second, academic self-efficacy is consistently associated with achievement-related behaviors and outcomes as discussed. Finally, there is reason to believe self-efficacy beliefs mediate the positive association seen earlier between faculty interactions, academic integration, and achievement for Black males (Santiago & Einarson, 1998). Therefore, since Black males tend to have lower levels of perceived self-efficacy that could explain the performance disparities of this subgroup in higher education. For Black males; however, the positive effects of self-efficacy beliefs may be moderated by their racial identity attitudes.

## IDENTITY

There is general consensus among researchers and theorists studying identity development that by adolescence, persons acquire an awareness of the attributes that distinguish groups (e.g., skin color, languages, and academic posture) and that inform opinions, behaviors and expectations about both their reference group and out-groups (Phinney, 1993; Rotheram-Borus et al., 1996). The strength of the peer or reference group to shape an individual's identity is related to the position of the reference group within the dominant culture (Ogbu & Simons, 1988). Minorities of color are typically not able to choose an identity, but rather are pressed to internalize one by societal signals due to experiences with, and perceptions about discrimination and prejudice (Phinney & Rosenthal, 1992). For a Black male, discriminatory behavior and attitudes from the broader society impose an identity that makes his race and gender salient to him (Phinney & Rosenthal, 1992). This salience in turn prescribes contextually acceptable behaviors: "High achievers often encounter difficulty integrating their social, racial, and academic identities" (Harper, 2010, p. 436). Even in late stages of adolescent development such as his college years, the African American male, similar to most students, seeks to adhere to a "role identity" that becomes the driver for present-day action (Dawson-Threat, 1997; Flores-Gonzalez, 2002), an identity that evolves with time.

The African American male's response to racial stimuli (Steele, 2003), his orientation toward large institutions such as his university, and his relations with others both within and outside his reference group could be shaped by progressive levels of sophistication along a racial identity range (Neville & Lilly, 2000). Helms (1990) amended Cross's (1971, 1978) five- stage racial identity model that he termed "nigrescence"—the process of becoming Black. In her formulation, each stage reflects attitudes along the continuum that represent a maturation process toward achieving a positive racial group orientation (Neville & Lilly, 2000). Blacks in the pre-encounter stage range from low-salience race-neutral individuals for which race plays an insignificant role in their everyday lives, to an anti-Black attitudinal pattern in which individuals have internalized racist stereotypes and have either actively abandoned Blacks as a reference group or behave in such a way as to hurt other Blacks (i.e., gang membership; Cross, 1991). The encounter stage is one in which a person begins to question his (or her) self-concept because of a dramatic event or series of experiences (Cross, 1971, 1978) that might occur in school, on the job, or an encounter with the penal system. The immersion/emersion stage is marked by an African American engaging himself in the Black experience and withdrawing from Whites as a means of formulating his new identity. His actions are considered severe and abrupt, and he is drawn to symbols of the new idealized identity (clothing, hairstyles, music) while rejecting representations associated with Whites and his old views. In the second phase of this stage, the Black male begins to experience an emersion or a leveling-off period from the emotionality, "either-or," blacker-than-thou mentality, catalyzed perhaps by a face-to-face encounter with a role model who exhibits a more advanced state of racial identity development. In the final internalization stage, a person resolves his conflicts with the old and new self and achieves a sense of inner security with his racial identity. His Blackness remains salient, but it is tempered by a more "open, expansive, and sophisticated" (Cross, 1991) conceptualization where he is willing to renegotiate his views and relations with members of other races. More settled in his identity, he can concentrate on meaningful activities that seek to benefit his reference group (commitment).

Racial identity attitudes, or variations in the stages of racial identity may explain why some African American males fail to engage with students of other races in predominantly White settings, while others maintain high levels of peer cohesion with White students and faculty (Davis et al., 2004). This study hypothesizes that the African American male who does well in predominantly White settings possesses an internalized racial identity that governs his ability to function within, and transition across school and home boundaries (Harper, 2010). What is known from racial identity theory is that Blacks who have resolved their racial identity no longer look solely to their reference group for appraisal but rather, they are motivated by what's uniquely best for them as individuals (Helms, 1990).

It is against these three conceptual backdrops—persistence, self-efficacy, and identity—that this study was conducted.

## PURPOSE

The study aims to answer the following question: Do successful African American male undergraduates in research PWIs also report heightened self-efficacy, racial identity attitudes, and levels of institutional integration? By integrating the theoretical domains institutional integration, academic self-efficacy, and racial identity theory, this study hopes to contribute to the literature by producing a multidimensional model for explaining the successful achievement of Black males.

## PROCEDURE

To answer the question, a statistical study was conducted to test the hypothesis that African American male undergraduates in predominantly White institutions who score higher on scales of self-efficacy, racial identity attitudes, and levels of institutional integration also score higher on measures of achievement. The aim of the design was to correlate the scale scores with cumulative GPAs of Black males enrolled full-time as sophomores and above attending research universities. The data were collected using a cross-sectional survey that comprised a battery of instruments and additional questions intended to solicit information about the parents, family, and academic performance of the respondents.

Three instruments were combined to create a 65-item Web-based questionnaire for this study. The Self-Efficacy for Academic Milestone Scale (AMS) developed by Lent, Brown, and Larkin (1986) rates confidence in students' ability to achieve specific academic objectives (i.e., "complete the requirements for your academic major with a grade point average of at least 3.0") consisting of 12 items rated on a 10-point scale, ranging from 0 (no confidence) to 9 (complete confidence) (Alpha ($\alpha$) ranges from .88 to .95, Hackett, Betz, Casas, & Rocha-Singh, 1992;) Lent, Brown, & Larkin, 1986). Several items were tailored to reflect the grading scale (4- or 5- point scale) and core institutional requirements for each university. In the current study, the subscale was very reliable ($\alpha$= .82).

The 30-item short form of the Black Racial Identity Attitude Scale (RIAS-B; Helms, 1990; Parham & Helms, 1981) is widely used for measuring Black racial identity of African American males and female college students (Abrams & Trusty, 2004; Campbell & Fleming, 2000; Cheatham, Slaney, & Coleman, 1990; Neville, Heppner, & Wang, 1997; Neville & Lilly, 2000; Nghe & Mahalik, 2001; Wilson & Constantine, 1999) originally defined by Cross (1971): pre- encounter, encounter, immersion/emersion, and internalization. Responses to the items ("I feel good about being Black, but do not limit myself to Black activities") are made on a 5-point Likert scale ranging from strongly disagree (1) to strongly agree (5). Psychometric analyses conducted on the short form yield reliability coefficients ranging from .50 for encounter, to .79 for internalization subscales (Helms, 1990). The present study yielded moderate to low reliability estimates on the four subscales: pre-encounter $\alpha$= .58), encounter $\alpha$= .44), immersion/emersion ($\alpha$= .69), and internalization ($\alpha$= .66). The encounter scale results were dropped from subsequent analyses because of its low reliability estimate.

To measure institutional integration, two subscales were used, peer-group interactions and interactions with faculty of the institutional integration scale (IIS), (Pascarella & Terenzini, 1980), a 34-item instrument that measures five facets of institutional integration. Responses to statements such as "Since coming here, I have developed close personal relationships with other students" and "Most of the faculty members I have had contact with are interested in helping students grow in more than just academic areas" were recorded on a 5-point scale with Likert-like response options ranging from 1 (strongly disagree) to 5 (strongly agree). Pascarella and Terenzini (1980) reported high reliability estimates of 0.84 and 0.83 for peer group interactions and interactions with faculty respectively. (Throughout this article, social integration refers to the peer group interaction scale, and academic interaction to the interactions with faculty scale.) Despite lower reliability coefficients than reported in the literature [peer group integration ($\alpha$= .72): interactions with faculty ($\alpha$= .52)], the high reliability measured by the authors on general college populations, and later confirmed by others for first-year students (French & Oakes, 2004) justified keeping the scale scores in the subsequent analysis.

In addition to the battery of existing instruments, several questions were provided to solicit information about the student's family background and high school and college performance. Responses to these questions supplied data for the key outcome variable (cumulative GPA) and control parameters (family income, parent education, and pre-college performance), all of which were critical for the subsequent analysis.

Five large research university members of the 94-member National Association of Multicultural Engineering Program Advocates (NAMEPA) were chosen as a convenience sample for this study. (A sixth institution offered to participate but was not selected because it was not a Research I university.) Table 1 presents the undergraduate enrollment and frequency of survey responses from each of the five institutions. Universities 1 and 2 are private research institutions located in the Northeast, while the remaining three are public universities. Two of the participating universities (Universities 4 and 5) are in the mid-Atlantic region, and University 3 is located in the Southwest.

**Table 1**

*Response Frequency by University*

| University (Undergraduate enrollment) | F | % | Cumulative % |
|---|---|---|---|
| University 1 (4,066) | 44 | 23.2 | 23.2 |
| University 2 (14,492) | 52 | 27.4 | 50.6 |
| University 3 (23,002) | 25 | 13.2 | 63.8 |
| University 4 (13,401) | 26 | 13.7 | 77.4 |
| University 5 (21,567) | 43 | 22.6 | 100.0 |
| Totals | 190 | 100.0 | |

The surveys were administered during the spring and summer semesters after the first examinations were administered on all campuses. Bandura (1986) maintained that self-efficacy ratings are most meaningful after the subjects receive feedback about recent performance. No incentives were offered to increase participation because of the anonymity of the respondents.

Of the 1,498 African American male sophomores and above who were invited to participate in the study by e-mail, a total of 201 students, or approximately 13 percent of the sample frame completed the survey. Freshmen were not included because they had not established a stable cumulative GPA and, in some cases, had not declared a major. Eleven cases were eliminated because they did not meet the sample criteria.

To allay concerns about response bias stemming from the low response rates, a *t*-test comparing the respondents to all Black males in the sample frame at one university (in which 23 percent responded since the researcher had access to all student-level data) revealed no significant difference in cumulative GPA [$t(163) = -.917$, $p = .36$], family income [$t(163) =.326$, $p =. 745$], and year in college [$t(149) = -1.103$, $p =. 272$], suggesting that the sample was representative of all Black males at that one institution. Because the researcher was not granted access to all student GPA, family income, and status data at the remaining four institutions, the $t$-test results were generalized to all participating universities, a limitation that is addressed later.

## DATA ANALYSIS

The variables used in the analysis are included in the Table 2. The responses were analyzed using SPSS 14 for Windows Graduate Student Version (Norusis, 2006).

A Pearson product-moment correlation analysis was run to estimate the strength and direction of the linear relationships between cumulative GPA, academic self-efficacy beliefs, levels of institutional integration, racial identity attitudes, and the control variables. Multiple regression analyses were conducted to estimate the strength and direction of the unique contribution of academic self-efficacy, racial identity subscale scores, and academic and social integration scores on cumulative GPA while controlling for all other factors listed in Table 2. Cumulative GPA was self-reported by the participant on a four-point scale. Five-point GPA scores were converted to the four-point scale. To mitigate the effects of grade variability across institutions, dummy variables for each institution were created. Also, two-way interactions were tested between several of the control and question variables. To estimate the final regression equation, a structured equation modeling method (Maximum Likelihood; Elisason, 1993) was used that first estimated the variables as a conceptual group (e.g., all racial identity subscale scores) to separately estimate the effects of each conceptual category on cumulative GPA.

# RESULTS

## DEMOGRAPHICS

The average respondent was almost a third of the way through his junior year (3.31 years) majoring in science (75 percent of the sample majored in at least one science, technology, engineering, or mathematics (STEM) discipline), earning a collegiate GPA of 2.97. He arrived at his university with a B+ average (unweighted high school GPA = 88.66) and a combined SAT score of about 1240, placing him nationally in the 84th percentile among SAT test takers (ACT, 2006; The College Board, 2000). His parents on average had attended some college while his mother had slightly more education (16.05) than his father (15.54). The average annual family income fell on the high end of the $25,000–$50,000 range.

## BIVARIATE ANALYSIS

Table 3 presents the means, standard deviations, and estimated bivariate correlations for all control and question variables measured in this study.

**The relationship among self-efficacy, racial identity, institutional integration and achievement.** Of the question variables, only academic self-efficacy ($r = .445$, $p < .001$) and academic integration ($r = .268$, $p < .001$) significantly correlated with collegiate GPA at the .05 level. This is a major finding that agrees with both Bandura (1997) and Tinto (1993), and also confirms a hypothesis of this study. African American male students who are confident and satisfied with their opportunities to interact informally with faculty (and who have closer ties with faculty) perform better than students less confident or who rate more poorly the quality of their interactions with faculty.

Table 2

*List of Variables for Data Analysis*

| Variable Name | Description |
|---|---|
| *Outcome Variable* | |
| CUMGPA | Cumulative GPA self-reported by the participant on a four-point scale. Five-point GPA scores were converted to the four-point scale. To mitigate the effects of grade variability across institutions, dummy variables for each institution were created (see below). |
| *Control Variables* | |
| YEAR | Participant's year in school. |
| HSGPA | Self-reported unweighted high school grade point average on a scale of 1 to 100. High school grades reported on a 4.0 scale were converted to the 100 point scale. |
| COMSAT | Self-reported combined score on highest SAT I (math and verbal) scores. Reported ACT scores were converted to SAT scores by comparing percentiles of English/Verbal and Mathematics scores. |
| INCOME | Ordinal variable of family income in $25,000 ranges (1 = <$25,000; 2=$25,000-$49,999; 3=$50,000-$74,999; 4= >$75,000) |
| EDLVL_H | A continuous variable representing the number of years of education achieved by the parent with most education. |
| University 1-5 | Dummy variables for each university to account for grade variation. |
| STEM | Dummy variable indicating whether a student majored in at least one Science, Technology, Engineering, or Mathematics discipline. |
| *Question Predictors* | |
| ASE | Measure of academic self-efficacy using the academic milestone self-efficacy scale (AMS). Scores were calculated by dividing the sum of the responses by 12 (the number of items). |
| PREENC | Racial identity attitudes of the four subscales scales (Pre-encounter, Encounter, |
| ENCTR | Immersion/Emersion, Internalization) using the short form of the Racial Identity |
| IMM-EM | Attitude Survey (RIAS-B). Scores are the mean of the responses for each subscale |
| INTERN | (PREENC:9 items; ENCTR:4 items; IMM-EM:8 items; INTERN:9 items). |
| AI | Measure of Academic Integration using the Institutional Integration Scale (IIS). The variable is calculated by averaging the scores over the five items after recoding negatively worded items. |
| SI | Measure of Social Integration using the Institutional Integration Scale (IIS). Scores were calculated (after recoding) by dividing the sum of the total by seven (items). |

Table 3

*Means, Standard Deviations, and Pearson Correlations for African American Males on Demographic, Performance, and Attitudinal Variables*

| | 1 | 2 | 3 | 4 | 5 | 6 | 7 | 8 | 9 | 10 | 11 | 12 | 13 |
|---|---|---|---|---|---|---|---|---|---|---|---|---|---|
| 1.Cumulative GPA | — | | | | | | | | | | | | |
| 2.Year in college | .085 | — | | | | | | | | | | | |
| 3.HS GPA | .262** | .066 | — | | | | | | | | | | |
| 4.Combined SAT | .398*** | -.083 | .411*** | — | | | | | | | | | |
| 5.Parent education level | .025 | -.009 | .110 | .353*** | — | | | | | | | | |
| 6.Family income | .052 | .028 | .004 | .134~ | .288*** | — | | | | | | | |
| 7.Self-efficacy | .445** | .142~ | .109 | .293*** | .079 | .002 | — | | | | | | |
| 8.Social integration | .084 | -.081 | .205* | .220* | .153* | .199** | .069 | — | | | | | |
| 9.Academic integration | .268*** | .072 | .098 | .141~ | -.024 | .040 | .182* | .259*** | — | | | | |
| 10.Pre-encounter | -.028 | .054 | -.004 | .035 | -.041 | .136~ | -.006 | -.008 | .061 | — | | | |
| 11.Immersion/Emersion | -.046 | -.072 | -.248** | -.227** | -.243** | -.233** | -.123~ | -.376*** | -.074 | -.181* | — | | |
| 12.Internalization | -.102 | -.093 | -.113 | -.225* | -.067 | -.128~ | -.129~ | -.006 | .004 | -.403*** | .471*** | — | |
| 13.STEM major | -.094 | .113 | .139~ | .179* | .039 | -.032 | -.001 | .002 | -.106 | -.021 | -.040 | -.014 | — |
| *M* | 2.97 | 3.31 | 88.66 | 1239.05 | 17.01 | 2.83 | 7.94 | 3.61 | 3.27 | 1.90 | 2.39 | 3.90 | .74 |
| *SD* | .53 | 1.09 | 9.21 | 149.97 | 3.29 | 1.11 | .97 | .69 | .69 | .48 | .60 | .51 | .44 |

*Note. M* = Mean; *SD* = Standard Deviation; ~*p* < .10; *\*p* < .05; *\*\*p* < .01; *\*\*\*p* < .001.

Moreover, Table 3 reveals a weak but positive and significant correlation between self- efficacy and academic integration ($r = .182$, $p = .013$), which could mean that confident students are more apt to approach faculty, or strong faculty ties increase academic confidence. The results suggest that that self-efficacy may facilitate the quality of faculty interaction. In addition to the positive link between academic self-efficacy, academic integration and GPA, combined SAT I score ($r = .398$, $p < .001$) and high school GPA ($r = .262$, $p < .001$) were also found to be positively linked to collegiate GPA, confirming earlier studies that revealed a link between certain pre-college preparation and college success (Bowen & Bok, 1998; Johnson, 1993; Strayhorn, 2010).

**Multiple regression analysis.** A systematically fitted taxonomy of nested multiple regression models was built containing control and question variables to estimate their effect on cumulative GPA. Table 4 contains the results of the multiple regression analysis of academic self-efficacy, institutional integration, and racial identity attitudes on academic achievement from the final fitted model. Forty-two percent of the variance in cumulative GPA is explained by this model [Adjusted $R2 = .372$, $F(11,158) = 9.492$, $p < .001$].

**Table 4**

*Multiple Regression Analysis of the Effects of Self-Efficacy, Institutional Integration, and Racial Identity Attitudes on Achievement of Black Males Attending Research Universities*

| Independent Variables | β | Beta | t | p |
|---|---|---|---|---|
| Constant | 3.609 | | 2.194 | .030 |
| STEM major | -.226 | -.187 | -2.83 | .005 |
| HS GPA | .012 | .205 | 2.83 | .005 |
| Combined SAT I scores | .001 | .274 | 3.60 | .000 |
| Academic self-efficacy | .169 | .291 | 4.34 | .000 |
| Social integration | -1.07 | -1.39 | -2.77 | .006 |
| Academic integration | -.067 | -.086 | -.308 | .758 |
| Immersion/Emersion (I/E) | .663 | .735 | 2.27 | .025 |
| Internalization | -1.55 | -1.47 | -3.39 | .001 |
| Social integration x Internalization | .261 | 1.60 | 2.68 | .008 |
| Academic integration x Internalization | .166 | 1.017 | 2.07 | .041 |
| Academic integration x I/E | -.181 | -.851 | -2.001 | .047 |

*Note. $R^2 = .415$; Adjusted $R^2 = .372$; $F(16,142) = 9.492$; $p < .001$*

**Significant main effects on achievement.** Echoing the results of the correlation analysis, as Table 4 indicates, the main effects of academic self-efficacy, combined SAT score, and high school GPA had a significant and positive influence on cumulative GPA while accounting for all other factors used in the model. Of these, Self-efficacy (Beta = .291, $t$ = 4.34, $p < .001$) and combined SAT score (Beta = .274, $t$ = 3.60, $p < .001$) had the strongest effect, followed by high school GPA (Beta = .205, $t$ = 2.83, $p$ =.005). Pertinent to the research question, the most academically successful Black males in college also scored higher on levels of self-efficacy, even after accounting for all other factors including their major, their high school GPA, parent income and education, and SAT scores. This supports the earlier correlation finding, but with statistical controls applied. In addition, Black males who come to the university with strong high school records and test scores are more likely to be the highest achievers. Neither income nor parent education factored into the equation.

New in this analysis is the influence of majoring in the life or physical sciences, mathematics, engineering or technology on GPA, which had a unique and weakly negative influence on achievement (Beta =-.187, $t$ = -2.833, $p$ = .005). On average, Black males in the STEM fields do more poorly than those majoring in non-STEM disciplines, holding other factors constant.

**Significant two-way effects on achievement.** A significant two-way interaction between internalization and social integration subscale scores (Beta =.160, $t$ = 2.68, $p$ =.008) was discovered, suggesting that social integration scores had a statistically different effect on GPA depending on the level of racial identity internalization. This is an important finding that confirms a hypothesis of this study, although the influence of the theorized relationship between internalization, social integration and achievement is less straightforward than originally predicted. An internalized African American male—one who has a positive and stable Black identity and who is more likely to have formed relationships that transcend race (Helms, 1990)—is associated with higher academic performance in PWIs.

Also discovered was a significant and positive two-way interaction between academic integration and internalization and GPA. The more racially internalized the African American male, the greater the influence on achievement of having meaningful and high-quality interactions with faculty and peers.

Finally, a significant two-way interaction was also discovered between the immersion/emersion subscale scores and academic integration, but the effect is the inverse of internalization as discussed earlier. In this instance, the quality of faculty interactions seems to have a moderate effect on the achievement of Black males who score higher on immersion/emersion scores. This important, and yet, complex relationship will be discussed in the next.

# DISCUSSION

### FACTORS THAT INFLUENCE ACHIEVEMENT
The major hypothesis of this study holds that Black males attending research universities who report heightened self-efficacy, positive racial identity attitudes, and high levels of institutional integration would earn higher cumulative GPAs. This was substantiated, although the results revealed greater complexity than hypothesized. Reflecting the findings of this study, a multi- dimensional achievement model (Figure 1) is proposed that depicts the influence of institutional integration, self-efficacy and racial identity attitudes on achievement.

**Self-efficacy.** High-achieving African American males report a heightened sense of self- efficacy, with this motivational belief having the strongest direct effect on achievement among all the factors considered (see figure Link B). The most academically successful African American males were also confident that they would be successful in college even after accounting for their SAT scores, high school grades, college major, and their parents' education and income (Table 3). This finding in part supports the main hypothesis and validates findings from several studies of college students that show academic self-efficacy to be a significant predictor of collegiate achievement (Bandura, 1997; Combs, 2001; Gainor & Lent, 1998; Pajares, 2002; Schunk, 1983). A relationship between Self-efficacy and academic integration also emerged.

**Self-efficacy and academic integration.** The most confident students also reported being satisfied with their opportunities to interact with their faculty (see figure Link C). This important finding has an explanation rooted in social cognitive theory. Verbal judgments from influential people are a source of self-efficacy as was discussed earlier. It is possible that as students interact favorably with their faculty, the instructors in turn convey their high expectations and affirm their intellectual abilities, thereby building their self-efficacy (Steele, 2003).

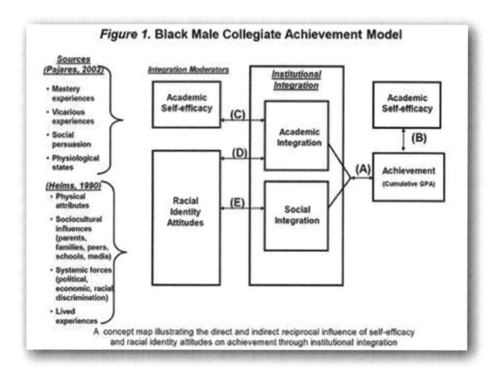

**Figure 1.** Black Male Collegiate Achievement Model

A concept map illustrating the direct and indirect reciprocal influence of self-efficacy and racial identity attitudes on achievement through institutional integration

An alternative explanation for the link between self-efficacy and faculty integration is also suggested in the literature. Efficacious students tend to exhibit assertive behaviors that may be an advantage in the college setting, particularly as they engage faculty (Gainor & Lent, 1998; Morris, 2004; Peterson, 1993; Phinney & Haas, 2003). Specifically, confident students could be more likely to approach their faculty than students less confident in their abilities.

These findings suggest that universities can directly improve the outcomes of African American males by raising their perceived levels of academic self-efficacy, which the literature suggests, by progressively providing mastery experiences, exposing them to success through vicarious experiences (i.e., role models), offering affirming verbal judgments (by way of mentors and teachers), and assessing and managing their physiological and emotional states perhaps with advising and counseling (Bandura, 1997; Morris, 2004; Pajares, 2002). Academic self-efficacy, therefore, plays a dual role in the model, both directly influencing achievement, and also correlating positively with the quality of faculty interactions. The more complex relationship between institutional integration and achievement than was hypothesized is discussed.

**Institutional integration, racial identity and achievement.** Black males with higher GPAs in college also report higher levels of faculty and social integration (see figure Link A), although the relationship is moderated by their racial identity attitudes (Links D and E). African American males who have a resolved and stable racial identity and who view their faculty and peer interactions favorably tend to do better in college than students who are less resolved in their racial identity who are also institutionally integrated. Moreover, holding strong pro-Black/anti-White attitudes mitigates the effect of greater faculty integration for Black males.

**Social integration and racial identity.** The literature provides key psychosocial insights into why the internalization attitude moderates social integration. The internalized ego stage has been empirically linked to higher psychological functioning (Brookins, Anyabwile &

137

Nacoste, 1996), positive self-concept (Wilson & Constantine, 1999), and goal-directed behavior (Jackson & Neville, 1998) which all have social implications. While the internalized African American male maintains identification with Blacks as his primary reference group, he also develops a concern for others with less regard to race or national origin and is more likely to have formed relationships that transcend race (Davis et al., 2004; Helms, 1990). Multicultural friendships of a Black male are associated with higher college satisfaction than for those having a mono-cultural friendship circle (Bowen & Bok, 1998).

Echoing an earlier study, Campbell (1996) offered another more practical explanation. An internalized racial identity attitude is positively linked to strong study habits. Consequently, it is plausible that students who had more pride and security in their identity interacted more favorably with a cross-section of students, picking up good learning habits along the way.

**Academic integration and racial identity.** As hypothesized, academic integration, or the quality of interaction with faculty, was significantly and positively associated with levels of achievement for Black males in this study. Generally, African American males who report stronger relationships with faculty ("since coming to this university, I have developed a close personal relationship with at least one faculty member") on average perform at higher levels (Table 3). This correlation empirically builds on one element of Tinto's (1993) Institutional Integration Theory, which maintains that the extent to which a student positively responds to the intellectual challenges of a university, and integrates into the institutional milieu, will be reflected in his persistence. These results also hold for African American males in the literature as well. For instance, both Davis (1994) and Allen (1992) discovered a link between achievement and academic integration for African American males attending both HBCUs and PWIs. Additionally, while Strayhorn (2008) found no link between supportive relationships and achievement, having a strong support person(s) was positively related with college satisfaction. In other words, by implication, Black males also benefit from greater faculty contact.

As the present study discovered, not all Black males benefit from higher perceived quality of faculty interactions (academic integration). For students who have a more internalized, positive racial identity, the effect of academic integration on achievement was greater than for African American males who had a less evolved racial identity. Referring to the latter, higher quality of faculty contact had a more moderate effect on achievement than for those students who had less racial maturity (immersion/emersion). Only Black males who had achieved a greater level of cultural fluency (internalization attitudes) benefited from meaningful faculty contact. Theoretically, these more internalized young men who were more stable in their identity would also be more cognitively and emotionally unburdened to concentrate on meaningful activities (Cross, 1991) such as making improvements in their study habits.

Given the intensity of emotions and pro-Black worldviews associated with the immersion/emersion stage and coupled with the resultant isolationist and often oppositional behaviors, it is plausible that the positive effect of improved faculty–student interaction is moderated by high immersion/emersion attitudes. Any faculty interaction could be viewed with skepticism by the Black male in this ego stage of his development.

To summarize, this study found no direct relationship between social integration and measures of achievement for Black males attending research universities except when their racial identity was considered. For Black males who are more racially resolved, there is a positive relationship between levels of social integration and academic achievement. The more successful students have a stable Black identity and high quality interactions with their peers (Dawson-Threat, 1997). These findings suggest that concerted efforts should be made to help Black males grow in their understanding of their own racial identity by fostering their growth from immersion to emersion, and eventually to internalization attitudes if they are to increase their performance and the quality of their college experience.

# LIMITATIONS

This study has several factors that may limit the generalizability of the findings. First, the sample of African American males is drawn from a convenience sample of institutions. Additionally, four of the five participating institutions were selective universities that admit less than 50 percent of its applicants. Future studies along this line of inquiry should consider a random selection of a broader array of institutions to ensure a more rigorous site sampling approach that includes both selective and non-selective research universities.

While this study theorized a direct relationship between institutional integration and achievement, the association was less straightforward than originally predicted. Only Black males who had achieved a greater level of cultural fluency (internalization attitudes) benefited from meaningful faculty and peer contact. Future research should incorporate qualitative research methods to surface why levels of integration were moderated by certain racial identity attitudes.

The research design could not rule out the possibility that there were systematic differences in unobservable traits (such as self-efficacy or racial identity attitudes) between responders and non-responders derived from the low survey response rates. However, to mitigate this possibility, differences in observable traits between responders and non-responders were tested at one institution where data were made available. Running similar tests at all five institutions would have ensured that representative samples of Black males were included in the analysis. Follow up studies might consider a research design to increase the response rates of this population. Perhaps by administering paper surveys during special or existing gatherings of students on campus, response rates would be sufficient to mitigate the need for the $t$-test analyses across all institutions.

This study relies on self-reported grade point averages for the dependent variable. Studies have shown high correlations of between .70 and .88 between self-reported and actual GPA for college students (Goldman, Flake, & Matheson, 1990). Future studies should secure access to actual grades from all participating institutions and thus potentially improve the strength of the resultant statistical analysis.

## CONCLUSION

A college degree is an essential key toward active participation in an increasingly global society (The College Board, 2010); however, African American males have been chronically underrepresented among college graduates, graduating at the lowest levels of all population segments. This study contributes to the literature by adding a psycho-social lens to Tinto's (1993) institutional integration theory that argues students who perceive high levels of institutional support, faculty contact, and social integration and who are in congruence with the mainstream of campus life are more likely to graduate. The findings suggest that in-college perceptions and experiences may interact with perceived self-efficacy and racial identity attitudes, which could lead certain African American males to respond differently to academic and social challenges on campus. In addition, it attempts to extend the discourse beyond simply persistence or surviving on campus, but rather to explain why African American males who have high grade point averages have achieved success.

These results suggest that predominantly White research universities can improve the outcomes of their Black male students by facilitating opportunities for them to meet and interact informally with university faculty. In parallel, institutions, and faculty in particular, can foster a climate that develops African American males' academic self-efficacy beliefs and racial identity in ways that avoid reifying a retreat into ideological and reference group isolation. One way to accomplish these objectives would be to establish seminars, facilitated discussion groups, or learning communities (Ross, 1998) in which peers can retreat into a place of "identity safety" (Steele, 2003), while fostering their connection with multicultural groups, faculty and administration. Through discussion and facilitating introductions to role models and mentors, students can catalyze their own developmental pathway from immersion to emersion, and ultimately to the internalization stage. One overarching goal would be to help the young Black men see that their academic pursuits and racial identity development are not orthogonal goals, thereby better positioning themselves for collegiate, economic, and professional success and civic engagement.

While the corpus of this article sheds light on how postsecondary institutions can improve completion rates of African American male undergraduates, a national campaign to improve the educational outcomes of African American boys earlier in the developmental pipeline is also essential if college-going rates are to dramatically increase (Palmer et al., 2010). Many of the lessons learned from this study about the need to facilitate institutional integration by leveraging self-efficacy beliefs and racial identity attitudes can and should be applied in elementary and secondary schools at scale in order for this country to remain economically competitive, and for this subpopulation to thrive.

# REFERENCES

Abrams, L., & Trusty, J. (2004). African Americans' racial identity and socially desirable responding: An empirical model. *Journal of Counseling & Development, 82*, 365-374.

ACT, I. (2006). *ACT national and state scores*. Retrieved from http://www.act.org/news/data/ 98/tl.html

Allen, W. R. (1992). The color of success: African American college outcomes at predominantly White and historically Black public colleges and universities. *Harvard Educational Review, 62*, 26-44.

Astin, A. W. (1993). *What matters in college: Four critical years revisited.* San Francisco: Jossey-Bass.

Baker, C. N. (2008). Under-represented college students and extracurricular involvement: The effects of various student organizations on academic performance. *Social Psychology of Education, 11*, 273-298.

Bandura, A. (1986). *Social foundations of thought and action.* Eaglewood Cliffs, NJ: Prentice Hall.

Bandura, A. (1997). *Self-efficacy: The exercise of control.* New York: Freeman.

Bandura, A., Barbaranelli, C., Caprara, G. V., & Pastorelli, C. (2001). Self-efficacy beliefs as shapers of children's aspirations and career trajectories. *Child Development, 72*, 187-206.

Board, The College (2000). *2000 SAT I test performance.* Retrieved from http://usfweb2.usf.edu/UGRADS/EANDT/sat_percentiles.htm

Board, The College (2010). *Education pays.* Retrieved from http://trends. collegeboard.org/ education_pays

Bonner, F. A., & Bailey, K. W. (2006). Enhancing the academic climate for African American college men. In M. J. Cuyjet (Ed). *African American men in college* (pp. 24-46). San Francisco, CA: Jossey-Bass.

Bowen, W. G., & Bok, D. (1998). *The shape of the river: Long-term consequences of considering race in college and university admissions.* Princeton, NJ: Princeton University Press.

Bowen, W. G., Chingos, M. M., & McPherson, M. S. (2009). Crossing the finishing line: Completing college at America's public universities. Princeton, NJ: Princeton University Press.

Brookins, C. C., Anyabwile, T. M., & Nacoste, R. (1996). Exploring the links between racial identity attitudes and psychological feelings of closeness in African American college students. *Journal of Applied Social Psychology, 26,* 243-264.

Brower, A. M., & Ketterhageng, A. (2004). Is there an inherent mismatch between how Black and White students expect to succeed in college and what their colleges expect from them? *Journal of Social Issues, 60,* 95-116.

Brown, O. B. (1995). *Debunking the myth: Stories of African-American university students.* Bloomington, IN: Phi Delta Kappa.

Campbell, D. B. (1996). *The fear of success and its relationship to racial identity attitudes and achievement behavior in Black males.* (Unpublished doctoral dissertation). City University of New York, New York.

Campbell, D. B., & Fleming, J. (2000). Fear of success, racial identity, and academic achievement in Black male college students. *Community Review, 18,* 5-18.

Cheatham, H. E., Slaney, R. B., & Coleman, N. C. (1990). Institutional effects on the psychosocial development of African-American college students. *Journal of Counseling Psychology, 37,* 453-458.

Coleman, J., Campbell, E., Hobson, C., McPartland, J., Mood, A., & Weinfeld, F. (1966).

Equality of Educational Opportunity. Washington, DC: Government Printing Office.

Combs, J. E. (2001). *Academic self-efficacy and the over prediction of African American college student performance.* (Unpublished doctoral dissertation). University of California, Santa Barbara, CA.

Cross, W. E. (1971). The Negro-to-Black conversion experience: Toward a psychology of Black liberation. *Black World, 20,* 13-27.

Cross, W. E. (1978). Models of psychological nigrescence: A literature review. *Journal of Black Psychology, 5,* 13-31.

Cross, W. E. (1991). *Shades of Black: Diversity in African-American identity.* Philadelphia: Temple University Press.

Cuyjet, M. J. (1997). African American men on college campuses: Their needs and their perceptions. In M. J. Cuyjet (Ed.), Helping African American men succeed in college (pp. 5-16). San Francisco, CA: Jossey-Bass.

Davis, J. E. (1994). College in Black and White: Campus environment and academic achievement of African American males. *The Journal of Negro Education, 63,* 620-633.

Davis, M., Dias-Bowie, Y., Greenberg, K., Klukken, G., Pollio, J. R., & Thomas, S. P. (2004). "A fly in the buttermilk": Descriptions of university life by successful Black undergraduate students at a predominantly White southeastern university. *The Journal of Higher Education, 75,* 420-445.

Dawson-Threat, J. (1997). Enhancing in-class academic experiences for African American men. In M. J. Cuyjet (Ed.), Helping African American men succeed in college (pp. 31-42). San Francisco, CA: Jossey-Bass.

Donovan, R. (1984). Path analysis of a theoretical model of persistence in higher education among low-income Black youth. *Research in Higher Education, 21,* 243-252.

Eccles, J. S. (1994). Understanding women's educational and occupational choices. *Psychology of Women Quarterly, 18,* 585-609.

Eliason, S. R. (1993). *Maximum Likelihood Estimation: Logic and practice.* (Sage University Paper series on quantitative applications in the social sciences, 07-096). Newbury Park, CA: Sage.

Flores-Gonzalez, N. (2002). *School kids/street kids: Identity development in Latino students.* New York: Teachers College Press.

French, B. F., & Oakes, W. (2004). Reliability and validity evidence for the institutional integration scale. *Educational and Psychological Measurement, 64,* 88-98.

Gainen, J. (1995). Barriers to success in quantitative gatekeeper courses. In R. J. Menges & M. D. Svinicki (Eds.), *Fostering student success in quantitative gateway courses* (Vol. 61, pp. 5-14). San Francisco, CA: Jossey-Bass.

Gainor, K. A., & Lent, R. W. (1998). Social cognitive expectations and racial identity attitudes in predicting the math choice intentions of Black college students. *Journal of Counseling Psychology, 45*, 403-413.

Goldman, B. A., Flake, W. L., & Matheson, M. B. (1990). Accuracy of college students' perceptions of their SAT scores and high school and college grade point averages relative to their ability. *Perceptual and Motor Skills, 70*, 514.

Hackett, G., Betz, N. E., Casas, J. M., & Rocha-Singh, I. A. (1992). Gender, ethnicity, and social cognitive factors predicting the academic achievement of students in engineering. *Journal of Counseling Psychology, 39*, 527-538.

Harper, S. R. (2006). Enhancing African American male student outcomes through leadership and active involvement. In M. J. Cuyjet (Ed.), *African American men in college* (pp. 68-94). San Francisco, CA: Jossey-Bass.

Harper, S. R. (2010). Peer support for African American male college achievement: Beyond internalized racism and the burden of "acting white." In S. R. Harper & F. Harris (Eds.), *College men and masculinities: Theory, research, and implications for practice* (pp. 337- 358). San Francisco, CA: Jossey-Bass.

Helms, J. E. (1990). Black racial identity theory. In J. E. Helms (Ed.), *Black and White racial identity: Theory, research, and practice* (pp. 9-32). Westport, CT: Praeger.

Herrnstein, R. J., & Murray, C. (1994). *The Bell Curve: Intelligence and class structure in American life*. New York: The Free Press.

Hrabowski, F., Maton, K. I., & Greif, G. L. (1998). *Beating the odds: Raising academically successful African American males*. New York: Oxford University Press.

Jackson, C. C. & Neville, H. A. (1998). Influence of racial identity attitudes on African American college students' vocational identity and hope. *Journal of Vocational Behavior, 53*, 97-113.

Johnson, R. E. (1993). *Factors in the academic success of African American college males*. (Unpublished doctoral dissertation). University of South Carolina, Columbia.

Jones, L. (2001). Creating an affirming culture to retain African-American students during the post-affirmative action era in higher education. In L. Jones (Ed.), *Retaining African Americans in higher education: Challenging paradigms for retaining students, faculty and administrators* (pp. 3-20). Sterling, VA: Stylus.

Knapp, L. G., Kelly-Reid, J. E., & Whitmore, R. W. (2006). *Enrollment in postsecondary institutions, fall 2004: Graduation rates, 1998 & 2001 cohorts; and financial statistics, fiscal year 2004*. Retrieved from http://nces.ed.gov/pubsearch/pubsinfo.asp?pubid=2006155

Laar, C. V. (2000). The paradox of low academic achievement but high self-esteem in African American students: An attributional account. *Educational Psychology Review, 12*, 33-61.

LaVant, B. D., Anderson, J. L., & Tiggs, J. W. (1997). Retaining African American men through mentoring initiatives. *New Directions for Student Services* (Vol. 80, pp. 43-53). San Francisco: Jossey-Bass.

Lent, R. W., Brown, S. D., & Larkin, K. C. (1986). Self-efficacy in the prediction of academic performance and perceived career options. *Journal of Counseling Psychology, 33*, 265-269.

Leppel, K. (2002). Similarities and differences in the college persistence of men and women. *The Review of Higher Education, 25*, 433-450.

Light, R. J. (2001). *Making the most of college: Students speak their minds.* Cambridge: Harvard University Press.

May, G. S. (2002). *A retrospective on undergraduate engineering success for underrepresented minority students* (A report produced under contract to the National Action Council of Minorities in Engineering, Inc.). Atlanta, GA: Georgia Institute of Technology.

Mayo, M. W., & Christenfeld, N. (1999). Gender, race, and performance expectations of college students. *Journal of Multicultural Counseling & Development, 27*, 93-104.

Moore, J. L. (2001). Developing academic warriors: Things that parents, administrators, and faculty should know. In L. Jones (Ed.), *Retaining African Americans in higher education: Challenging paradigms for retaining students, faculty and administrators* (pp. 77-90). Sterling, VA: Stylus.

Morris, L. V. (2004). Self-efficacy in academe: Connecting the belief and the reality. *Innovative Higher Education, 28*, 159-162.

Neville, H. A., Heppner, P. P., & Wang, L.-f. (1997). Relations among racial identity attitudes, perceived stressors, and coping styles in African American college students. *Journal of Counseling & Development, 75*, 303-311.

Neville, H. A., & Lilly, R. L. (2000). The relationship between racial identity cluster profiles and psychological distress among African American college students. *Journal of Multicultural Counseling & Development, 28,* 194-207.

Nghe, L. T., & Mahalik, J. R. (2001). Examining racial identity statuses as predictors of psychological defenses in African American college students. *Journal of Counseling Psychology, 48,* 10-16.

Noguera, P. A. (2003). Joaquin's dilemma: Understanding the link between racial identity and school-related behaviors. In M. Sadowski (Ed.), *Adolescents at school: Perspectives on youth, identity, and education* (pp. 19-30). Cambridge, MA: Harvard Education Press.

Norusis, M. J. (2006). *SPSS 14.0 guide to data analysis.* Berkeley, CA: Prentice Hall.

O'Connor, C. (1997). Dispositions toward (collective) struggle and educational resilience in the inner city: A case analysis of six African American high school students. *American Educational Research Journal, 34,* 593-629.

Ogbu, J. U. (1990). Minority education in comparative perspective. *The Journal of Negro Education, 39,* 45-60.

Ogbu, J. U., & Simons, H. D. (1988). Voluntary and involuntary minorities: A cultural- ecological theory of school performance with some implications for education. *Anthropology of Education Quarterly, 29,* 1-24.

Pajares, F. (2002). *Overview of social cognitive theory and of self-efficacy.* Atlanta: Emory University Press.

Palmer, R. T., Davis, R. J., Moore III, J. L., & Hilton, A. A. (2010). A nation at risk: Increasing college participation and persistence among African American males to stimulate U.S. global competitiveness. *Journal of African American Males in Education, 1*, 105-124.

Palmer, R., & Gasman, M. (2008). "It takes a village to raise a child": The role of social capital in promoting academic success for African American men at a Black college. *Journal of College Student Development, 49*, 52-70.

Palmer, R. T., & Young, E. M. (2009). Determined to succeed: Salient factors that foster academic success for academically unprepared Black males at a Black college. *Journal of College Student Retention, 10*, 465-482.

Parham, T. A., & Helms, J. E. (1981). The influence of Black students' racial identity attitudes on preference for counselor's race. *Journal of Counseling Psychology, 28*, 250-257.

Pascarella, E. (1985). Racial differences in factors associated with bachelor's degree completion: A nine-year follow-up. *Research in Higher Education, 23*, 351-373.

Pascarella, E., Smart, J., Ethington, C., & Nettles, M. (1987). The influence of college on self- concept: A consideration of race and gender differences. *American Educational Research Journal, 24*, 49-77.

Pascarella, E. T., & Terenzini, P. T. (1980). Predicting freshman persistence and voluntary dropout decisions from a theoretical model. *The Journal of Higher Education, 51*, 60-75.

Pascarella, E. T., & Terenzini, P. T. (1991). *How college affects students.* San Francisco: Jossey-Bass.

Perry, T., Steele, C., & Hilliard, A. (2003). *Young, gifted, and Black: Promoting high achievement among African-American students.* Boston: Beacon Press.

Peterson, S. (1993). Career decision-making self-efficacy and institutional integration of underprepared college students. *Research in Higher Education, 34,* 659-685.

Phinney, J. S. (1993). A three-stage model of ethnic identity development in adolescence. In M. E. Bernal & G. P. Knight (Eds.), *Ethnic identity: Formation and transmission among Hispanics and other minorities* (pp. 61-79). Albany: State University of New York Press.

Phinney, J. S., & Haas, K. (2003). The process of coping among ethnic minority first-generation college freshmen: A narrative approach. *Journal of Social Psychology, 143,* 707-726.

Phinney, J. S., & Rosenthal, D. A. (1992). Ethnic identity in adolescence: Process, context, and outcome. In G. R. Adams, T. P. Gulotta & R. Montemayor (Eds.), *Adolescent identity formulation* (pp. 145-172): Sage.

Ross, M. J. (1998). *Success factors of young African-American males at a historically Black college.* Westport, CT: Bergen & Garvey.

Rotheram-Borus, M. J., Dopkins, S., Sabate, N., & Lightfoot, M. (1996). Personal and ethnic identity, values, and self-esteem among Black and Latino adolescent girls. In B. J. R.

Leadbeater & N. Way (Eds.), *Urban girls: Resisting stereotypes, creating identities* (pp. 35- 52). New York: New York University Press.

Santiago, A. M., & Einarson, M. K. (1998). Background characteristics as predictors of academic self-confidence and academic self-efficacy among graduate science and engineering students. *Research in Higher Education, 39,* 163-198.

Saunders, M. G. (1998). Overcoming obstacles: Academic achievement as a response to racism and discrimination. *The Journal of Negro Education, 66,* 83-93.

Schunk, D. S. (1983). Ability versus effort attributional feedback: Differential effects on self- efficacy and achievement. *Journal of Educational Psychology, 75,* 848-856.

Special report: College degree awards: The ominous gender gap in African-American education. (1999). *The Journal of Blacks in Higher Education, 23,* 6-9.

Steele, C. (2003). Stereotype threat and student achievement. In T. Perry, C. Steele & A. Hilliard (Eds.), *Young, gifted, and Black: Promoting high achievement among African- American students* (pp. 109-130). Boston: Beacon Press.

Stipek, D. J. (1984). The development of achievement motivation. *Research on Motivation in Education, Student Motivation, Volume 1,* 145-173.

Strayhorn, T. L. (2008). The role of supportive relationships in facilitating African American males' success in college. *NASPA Journal, 44,* 26-48.

Strayhorn, T. L. (2010). When race and gender collide: Social and cultural capital's influence on the academic achievement of African American and Latino males. *The Review of Higher Education, 33,* 307-332.

Sutton, E. M., & Terrell, M. C. (1997). Identifying and developing leadership opportunities for African American men. In M. J. Cuyjet (Ed.), *Helping African American men succeed in college* (pp. 55-64). San Francisco, CA: Jossey-Bass.

Thile, E. I., & Matt, G. E. (1995). The ethnic mentor undergraduate program: A brief description and preliminary findings. *Journal of Multicultural Counseling & Development, 23*, 116-126.

Tinto, V. (1993). *Leaving college: Rethinking the causes and cures of student attrition* (2nd ed.). Chicago, IL: University of Chicago Press.

U.S. Department of Education, National Center for Education Statistics. (Fall 2009) *Integrated Postsecondary Education Data System (IPEDS): Completions component.* Washington, DC: USDE.

U.S. Department of Education, National Center for Education Statistics. (Spring 2010a). *Integrated Postsecondary Education Data System (IPEDS). Enrollment component.* Washington, DC: USDE.

U.S. Department of Education, National Center for Education Statistics. (Spring 2010b). *Integrated Postsecondary Education Data System (IPEDS), Graduation rates component.* Washington, DC: USDE.

Why the large and growing gender gap in African-American higher education? (1998). *The Journal of Blacks in Higher Education, 19*, 34-35. Wilson, J. W., & Constantine, M. G. (1999). Racial identity attitudes, self-concept, and perceived family cohesion in black college students. *Journal of Black Studies, 29*, 354-366.

Wilson, W. J. (Ed.). (1996). *Ghetto-related behavior and the structure of opportunity.* New York: Knopf.

# INDEX

Made in the USA
Columbia, SC
23 June 2017